A Man, A Bike,
Alone Through Scotland

A Man, A Bike, Alone Through Scotland

by Eugene Cantin

World Publications

Box 366, Mountain View, CA 94042

"Voyaging is victory"
Arab proverb

Thoughts on Which to Travel

By all rights I had achieved the Great American Dream. I was practicing my profession—I teach tennis—10 hours a day, six days a week, at a new tennis club full of enjoyable people in the San Francisco Bay Area. I was making—for me—a great deal of money. Yet one afternoon, during my 14th lesson of the day, as young Master Everready hit another line drive over the side fence of the teaching court, a thought came to me. If this were the last year of my life, would I spend it this way? Ducking another shot off the wood, the answer came clearly: no. How would I spend it? Well, I'd always wanted to take a long bike trip somewhere, perhaps through Scotland. And it would be nice to travel with friends in Europe. And I did want to make that trek to Everest.

Then, as always happens eventually, Master Everready made the proper connections between eye, mind and body, and hit a perfect topspin backhand. A surge of pleasure rushed through this harried teacher. But I still found myself wondering, what would a bike trip through Scotland be like . . . ?

Henry Moore's King and Queen.

Contents

One
Preparations

I found myself shivering as I walked up Edinburgh's Leith Street. It was about 10 o'clock in the evening of a cold night in late March, and a thick, damp mist hung in the air, giving the yellow street lights a strange, haloed look. There was not much traffic, but I still had to be careful to look in all directions at each intersection. In Scotland the cars, with their right-hand drive, seemed to spring out of nowhere.

I turned onto Princes Street, Edinburgh's main shopping boulevard, and hurried along it. On my left, I passed the train station where I had first arrived in Edinburgh two hours before. Farther down from the station I could make out the bulk of the city's great castle looming through the shifting mist, while nearer at hand a monument to Sir Walter Scott stood like a black rocket about to blast away. On my right the street was lined with brightly lit store windows, their interiors a warm and inviting contrast to the chilling mist outside.

My arrival in Great Britain coincided with the height of the world gas crisis, and came just after the end of the three-day work week, which was forced on Britain by a coal miners' strike. While in the States, I had read accounts of how difficult it was to find bicycles for sale in Britain under these circumstances, that far fewer than normal had been produced and that those few available all were in high demand due to the gas crunch. Because of this information I wrote to the Scottish Tourist Board in Edinburgh. They replied with the name Halfords, and I next contacted them, asking if they could provide me with a touring cycle.

"Certainly, Mr. Cantin," came back their reply. "We can supply whatever cycle you may need."

With such a reassuring response in hand I left home, and while in London did not even bother looking over what selection of cycles might be available there. I was confident that Halfords could equip me, and now I was hurrying through the cold Edinburgh night to take a look through their window at their cycling selection.

As soon as I reached Halfords I knew that I was in trouble. Halfords is a very nice sort of store I am sure—just as a Sears or a Grand Auto is a nice store. But Halfords was nothing like the bike shop that I was hoping to find waiting for me. There were several bikes hanging in the dripping window, surrounded by auto seat covers and rear view mirrors, but none of them were the sort of light weight touring cycle I expected to find—had to find. The bikes on display were all inexpensive children's bikes, the sort a person might pick up during those last frenzied moments of shopping before Christmas. I knew that I was unfamiliar with long-distance cycling, but even *my* limited knowledge included an image of how a proper touring cycle should look. And Halfords had nothing that filled that image.

It was a long walk back to my guest house, allowing me lots of time to ponder the question of how one goes about taking a bike trip without a bike.

The next morning offered a warmer, brighter impression of Edinburgh as I retraced my steps of the night before. The cold mist was gone, the sun was trying to shine and the streets were filled with Edinburgh's smartly dressed citizens, hurrying about their affairs. Where the night before Edinburgh Castle had appeared as an ominous mass against the skyline, it now stood revealed as a fairy-tale castle, green lawns surrounding sheer rock walls that rose to a complicated jumble of turreted buildings that simply reeked with history.

As I walked along I could feel my spirits revive. After all, the man who had answered my query to Halfords was awfully confident. Perhaps they would be able to fill my needs. The upstairs of the Halfords' store promised more than what I had seen through the window downstairs. There were bikes lined up, and several of them looked closer to what I wanted. At least they did at a distance. As soon as I walked up to what seemed to be likely candidates for purchase, however, they instantly shrank to a small child's proportions, far too small for my use.

Before arriving in Edinburgh, I had held a mental image of simply walking into the best bike shop in town, selecting the perfect model and size for my needs and perhaps covering the first 50 miles of my trip that same day. Now I knew it wasn't going to be quite so easy.

I asked the girl behind the desk for the manager, the man who had answered my letter. A few minutes later he came upstairs.

"Yes," he said, "we are a little short on bikes in the larger sizes, the three-day work week, you know." Nonetheless, he assured me that he

3

would contact the other Halfords branches, and that he would be able to have two full-sized models for my inspection the following day. That sounded fine. I then asked if there happened to be any other bike shops nearby.

"Well, you might try MacDonald's," the manager answered doubtfully. "It's over on Bread Street."

As I had nothing better to do, I wandered over to Bread Street, on the far side of Castle Hill. MacDonald's Bike Shop was a small place, a narrow hole in the wall, and exactly what I had expected Halfords to be. The window was filled with hanging cycles, definitely of the racing/touring type I had in mind, and dozens of cycle parts and accessories also were littered about. Small boxes held Campagnolo derailleurs, Weinmann center-pull brakes, lights, toe clips and every other bike part you might think of. Of course, the bikes in the window were clearly too small, as were those at Halfords. Another drawback was that MacDonald's Bike Shop was securely closed behind a metal gate.

I spent the afternoon going through Edinburgh's Castle, marveling at the site high over Edinburgh that had seen and played an active part in well over a thousand years of Scottish history. When I thought enough time had passed, I hurried back to MacDonald's cyclery, but it was still firmly shut. With that I returned to Halfords, and talked once again with the manager, getting down to the details of purchasing a cycle from him. I left with the understanding that he would definitely have two bikes for my inspection by the following morning, and I implied that I would purchase one of them—if they were at all adequate.

The next morning I returned to Halfords.

"I'm terribly sorry," the manager said, "the bike hasn't arrived yet, but it will be here shortly. It's a 22½-inch bike."

What had happened to the *two* bikes, I wondered? And 22½ inches? That was absurd. A cycle's size is measured from the main horizontal bar of the frame down to the pedal hub, and 22½ inches would be just about right for a person standing 5 feet 8. I'm a little over 6 feet 3. But "beggars can't be choosers" I thought, and went off to kill time until the cycle made its appearance.

I spent my time walking back to Bread Street, to try MacDonald's again. This time the bike shop was open. Inside, I found the proprietor, a man with the euphonious name of Mr. Ronald MacDonald, happily dispensing information and equipment to a surprising crowd of customers, considering the tiny amount of room available in his cramped business space.

Mr. MacDonald was a man in his early 40s, bright-eyed, and obviously

Mr. MacDonald happily dispensed information and equipment to crowds of customers.

enthusiastic and knowledgeable about the sport that was his profession. When I finally made it to the head of the line of customers and explained the state of my search for a cycle, his response to Halfords' 22½-inch frame was immediate.

"Ach, ya dinna want something tha' small," he said. "It willna do!" You really should have a cycle with at least a 25½-inch frame, he said.

Did he have any, I asked?

Well, no, not just yet. The three-day work week, you know. But he did have some Carlton Continentals on order, just the thing for me. He expected them in at any time, he said, and promised to phone the factory for me during his lunchbreak that very afternoon, to see if they were coming in.

With that I went back to Halfords, and found that their offering had arrived for inspection. A tiny bike, I felt like a man on a mule when I got on it, my knees practically scraping the ground once I was aboard. Undaunted by my obvious lack of enthusiasm, the Halfords people assured me that all that was needed was a seat with a longer stem, which they immediately began to search for on the other bikes.

I promised to come back after lunch, and slipped away to call Mr. MacDonald.

"Well," he said, "the bikes are on the way, but no one knows for sure when they will get here. They should arrive in the next few days, though."

After a long lunch in a tea shop on Frederick Street, I went back to Halfords. I felt quite trapped by the indefinite arrival time of Mr. MacDonald's cycles. By now the busy Halfords' personnel had transformed a tiny bike, with too short a seat stem, into a tiny bike with an absurdly long seat stem. Overcome by their pride in their creation, I took the cycle out to the alley behind their shop and rode precariously up and down several times. It wasn't very comfortable, all cramped up atop that seat like a wavering tower, but I began to wonder what else I could do other than buy the cycle and try to make do. Finally, taking the coward's way out, I gave Halfords a firm "maybe," and hurried back to Mr. MacDonald's.

"Mr. MacDonald," I pleaded, "don't you have anything that might be better than a 22½-inch cycle? Do you happen to have any frames lying about?" I wasn't quite on the floor, hands clasped before me, but it was close. (As I was leaving Halfords, they informed me that they had not only called Glasgow, but also the Raleigh factory in Nottingham as well. The next cycles that they could expect of the proper size definitely would be arriving within 17 weeks—"The three-day work week, you know.")

But then bright-eyed Mr. MacDonald beamed at me and said, "Frames? Of course I have frames, lad."

"You do?" I excitedly asked. "You mean you have a frame that would be the right size? Here? Now?"

"Oh, yes," Mr. MacDonald replied, and he scuttled down into his heaped basement and returned a moment later with a boxed frame to prove it, saying, "I can *build* you a bike if you want. I just didn't know that you'd care to spend that kind of money. It will cost you more for me to build you a bike, you know."

At this point, I didn't really care how much the bike might cost, just

6

so I could lay my hands on one and get on my way.

"Let's explore the possibility," I said. As it turned out, Mr. MacDonald would undertake to build me a cycle of the proper size, with far better derailleur and brake equipment, for about 10 pounds (roughly $24) more than the cost of the cycle I had been shown at Halfords.

I couldn't agree fast enough. Mr. MacDonald hastened to point out that he couldn't hope to have the cycle finished before the following Monday. It was now Thursday. As I was completely overjoyed at finding a cycle at all, this hardly seemed a drawback. Next we worked through the list of parts I wished to have on the machine.

"Ten gears?" he asked. "Ya dinna need 10 gears, not if you're fit, man," and so on.

At last I thanked him, and hurried off to give Halfords a final and definite no. I was sorry about the work they had gone to on my behalf— even if their end result was a monster—and was grateful when they took my final refusal quite calmly.

I spent the next few days taking in some of the sights of Edinburgh, as well as thinking about the trip to come. The longest trip I had ever made aboard a cycle before this was one of 23 miles around the Point Reyes National Seashore in California. Now I found myself strolling about an ancient city in a foreign land, waiting for my personal cycle to be constructed by a skilled craftsman, so that I might launch myself out on what I vaguely imagined to be a trip circling Scotland's entire coastline. I really had no more detailed plan than that—and even this vague plan was dropped when I finally took a good look at a map of Scotland and saw just how much coastline there actually was. What I was seeking was a change from my pursuits of the previous year, and even a mostly planless bike trip through Scotland seemed just the ticket.

Before coming to Scotland I browsed through maps of the country, and found myself fascinated by the rolling names that leaped off them at me: Wigtown, the Grampian Mountains, Loch Snizort, Lairg and Loch Shin, Glen Affric, Ben Bui, the Island of Egg, Mid-Lothian, the Lammermuir Hills. All of these and thousands more seemed to be calling, summoning me in strident tones. Scotland: A whole country, small enough that one could seriously try to see all of it. Yet large enough that there would always be something new over the next hill. No wonder I was excited.

I planned to stay in bed and breakfast establishments while I traveled, or possibly in the youth hostels that are liberally sprinkled throughout Scotland. I had encountered bed and breakfasts—or B&Bs, as they are known—in England on an earlier trip, and knew what an excellent value they were. At B&Bs you sleep in a private home, and enjoy a large breakfast for a price well under that charged by normal hotels. You are treated as a guest in these places, and no matter how small the home, you usually have your own room.

You also get a feeling of community in a B&B that you wouldn't find in a hotel, particularly if your hosts serve a complimentary "tea" in the evening. These evening teas are not really part of the price you pay at a B&B, so it was always exciting each evening that I stayed at one to see what sort of tea might be served, or if any would be served at all.

B&Bs are unique to Great Britain, as far as I've seen, which is too bad. They provide a very nice way for travelers to enjoy inexpensive food and lodging. In Scotland the B&Bs are very well organized to accommodate visitors, with local tourist boards throughout the country providing accommodation booklets telling where the B&Bs are located and what they offer.

At last it was Monday. Late that afternoon I walked back to Bread Street to take possession of my intended two-wheeler. I had noticed that Mr. MacDonald had a remarkable capacity for long, friendly conversations with each of his customers, so I was not surprised to find my cycle unfinished, still hanging on an assembly mount. Mr. MacDonald talked as he worked, explaining just what he was doing, enthusiastically assuring me the cycle would surely carry me anywhere I might want to go.

The cycle was beautiful, lean, efficient. It was truly a machine to carry you to the ends of the world. Bigger than any cycle I had ever seen before, this Carlton Grand Prix was also the most eye-pleasing I had ever seen. The dark blue and black frame was accented by bands of gold, with its brand

Looking down Princess Street in Edinburgh.

name the same color, contrasting nicely with the yellow and black high-pressure tires. The whole was topped with down-turned, white-taped handlebars and a high black seat.

The beauty of my cycle was not limited just to its visual appearance. The derailleur, the mechanism that changes the position of the drive chain on the block of five—"Ya dinna need ten!"—gears on the rear wheel, was a Sun Tour G.T. derailleur. A bit of reading informed me that this was considered the finest derailleur after the absurdly expensive, but very excellent, touring model produced by Campagnolo. The brakes were center-pull Weinmann 999 Vainquers, once again an excellent brand. Mr. MacDonald assured me the Carlton frame was certainly as good a touring frame as I might find anywhere for the price. In all, I could only be happy with the prospect of riding such a glorious creation.

Mr. MacDonald gave the tires a final pumping with the white plastic hand pump that rode just under the horizontal bar of the frame, then with a smile told me to take a spin around the block before he closed for the night.

The cycle flew down Lady Lawson Street, over Spittal Street, and back to Bread Street like a dream. I fumbled a bit with the gears, very glad to have only 5 rather than 10 with which to become confused. Under me, the cycle was sure and silent. It was wonderful to be stretched out comfortably from seat to handlebars, unlike the scrunched-up position I assumed on the much-too-small offering from Halfords.

Mr. MacDonald made a final check of my machine, handed me an all-purpose wrench, two tire irons and a patch kit, and with a handshake sent me on my way. I swooped down West Port, but ended walking the bike up Grassmarket and down High Street as I found I couldn't deal comfortably with the cobblestones used in these streets. It was almost dark as I flew down North Bridge and Leith Streets—both macadamized. (Macadam, by the way, was invented by John McAdam, born in Ayr in 1756.)

In a few minutes I was back at my guest house, and safely carried the cycle down to my room. Even resting against the wall the cycle appeared to be flashing along through space. A beautiful machine, I thought again, worthy of the venture I planned.

I had in my luggage three nylon bike bags, and I was going to carry only essentials in them—two heavy Nikon bodies, wide angle and zoon lenses, 30 rolls of film, a three-man tent, sleeping bag, rain gear and, out of habit, a tennis racket and proper clothing for that sport, not to mention a tripod, and my boots. Very quickly the cycle was on the point of disappearing under a great ziggurat of bike bags, stuff bags and tent bags.

9

The bike seemed to groan under the weight. Somewhere I had heard that Scotland might offer one or two hills over which I would somehow have to transport all that junk. With a bit of rationalization the boots and tent became less essential to the operation. That saw 10 pounds removed from the tottering pile. I expected to carry the racket and tennis clothes only through my first swing south of Edinburgh and then back up to Glasgow. (I had heard of a tournament that I might be able to play in that city.) Perhaps I didn't need a second camera body for black and white film, or the wide-angle lens. There went another two to three pounds. Things were looking up.

I have a terrible weakness for anthropomorphizing the objects around me. In other words, I like to give them names. Having finished packing, I found myself leafing through the excellent miniature guide to Scotland that I planned to use (*The Blue Guide*, put out by the Benn Company of London, unfortunately now out of print, but perhaps soon to return), and discovered a section just after a list of the "Rulers of Scotland" and just before the "Glossary of Gaelic Roots," titled "Glossary of Lowland Scots."

"Well now," I thought, "how about naming this cycle? What could be better than a proper Scottish name?" With that I ran through the list of Scottish words, and ended with a toss-up between *Braw Handsel* and *Huntygowk*. The first translated as "Handsome Gift of Luck," the *Blue Guide* told me, while the second meant "Fool's Errand." I was attracted by the noble sound of a word like *Huntygowk*, but as it seemed unwise to start off on a trip aboard a "Fool's Errand," I ended by settling for the other.

"Braw Handsel is your name, bike," I announced to the inanimate object against the wall. "And may you indeed be a 'Gift of Luck.' "

The only problem with such an act is that the object so named may immediately take it into its head to develop a character to go along with— or in opposition to—its given name. Now, it may be that Braw Handsel in fact had his heart and soul set on being announced to the world as *Huntygowk*, or perhaps he wished to go by another name entirely. Perhaps Braw Handsel was by nature a Highland cycle, in which case my giving it a Lowland name would be the worst mistake imaginable.

In any case, I swear that that beautiful, inanimate object, from the moment I named it Braw Handsel, began to develop the craftiest, most cunning, most dastardly and awkward character of any object I have ever made sentient. Of course, I know perfectly well that my Carlton Grand Prix 25½-inch frame, with center-pull Weinmann 999 Vainquer caliper brakes and Sun Tour G.T. derailleur, mounted on Dunlop high-pressure tubes remained just this assemblage of objects and nothing more. Nevertheless, part of me declares that the cycle was alive and keenly aware of its powers and prerogatives.

Inanimate object versus cunning opponent. I can't decide the matter. I leave it up to you to decide. For my part, I had a bike named Braw Handsel. It was early morning when I retired for some rest before the start of my first cycling trip in a foreign country.

Two
The First Day

The next morning I reeled off 75 miles before lunchtime, because of my superb physical condition and lightning reflexes. That, at least, is what I would like to report. Unfortunately, such a report would be a lie. I did wake earlier than usual, but found myself reluctant to leave the warmth and comfort of my lodgings. Faced with all the unknowns of a major trip, I seemed to prefer to stay in bed.

At last the demands of impending adventure got me up, and I carried the loaded cycle upstairs—a neat trick in the narrow and turning stairwell—in order to give it a road test on the broad London Road just outside my B&B. As I rode along I found myself muttering, "Stay to the left, stay to the left!" to try to cope with the alien traffic patterns. I also found myself tipping over a lot. It was surprising—at least to an amateur such as myself—just how different a loaded cycle is from an unloaded one. The loaded cycle has a mind of its own, and tends to want to continue in nice, straight, upright lines rather than leaning and turning swiftly the way an unloaded one does. This discovery dictated a return to my room and further work at paring down the overweight. (Despite my efforts, though, I think I carried about 35 pounds of dunnage, much too much.) Then came a long and relaxing hotel breakfast—the usual B&B meal of cereal, toast, ham and eggs and gallons of tea. Finally, I could find nothing further to dawdle over, so I thanked Mr. O'Connell for taking care of my unneeded luggage and bade him good-bye.

It was 11 o'clock when I finally began to pedal my way through the maze of streets behind Castle Hill that led to larger main roads out of Edinburgh. The sun was shining, and it certainly was not an unpleasant day for a bike ride. The going was slow at first, but I hardly noticed, excited as I now was at the thought ringing in my mind, "Here we go at last!"

Beyond Clerk Street I found myself heading down a gentle slope, working through the gears on the cycle, enjoying the speed and wind blowing past me. Racing along, trying to keep clear of the trucks and cars that whipped by, I almost failed to notice something very common to European cities, but rare in America. Outside Edinburgh there is an abrupt departure from the city to the surrounding countryside, with hardly any transition at all. In almost a single instant, the smog and sounds of the city gave way to earthier farm smells and the sounds of grazing animals. Instead of office buildings and rows of homes, I found myself surrounded by fields stretching off into the distance, neatly divided by endless stone walls. As I made that rapid transition from the cosmopolitan city of Edinburgh to the truly Scottish countryside that surrounds it, I felt a sudden wave of fresh exuberance surge over me. I was in Scotland, and embarking upon a bike journey that up until now had been just a vague idea in my mind. Now that journey was no longer expectation. It had begun for real.

Despite my pleasant country surroundings, I had to keep more attention on the road and its fast-moving traffic than I really wished to. Once outside Edinburgh I was on a two-lane road, but the cars and massive trucks did not seem to slow down or get any smaller for all that. The British employ diesel trucks just as large as those in the States, and British motorists who must deal with these mobile monstrosities have adopted the perfect name for them—juggernauts. I quickly came to dread the passage of these trucks as they rocketed by on narrow roads. Their airstreams first tended to blow me off the road, and then tried to suck me back into the trucks' sterns. It was quite unnerving to be whipped back and forth as these iron-clad behemoths rushed by. After experiencing the passage of several juggernauts, I formulated a rule that I adhered to throughout the trip: If you have a choice, opt for quiet, scenic back roads.

Spring weather had not reached Scotland yet, this early in April. Although the fields were green with short blades of new grass, the trees along the road were still gnarled and leafless, excepting the scattered evergreens that added their full green hues to the surroundings.

The road varied considerably, from long open-country stretches to narrow, twisting lanes. The country on each side was divided into fields neatly framed by stone walls, hedgerows or higher walls of living trees. The fields seemed of a very human size, much smaller than the endless expanses common to the States.

Everywhere there seemed a great sense of life, of spring beginning to stir beneath the surface. In one field a new-born lamb, still red from its mother's womb, was actively butting her undercarriage in search of milk.

13

On the fringes of other fields rabbits hopped about in search of edibles, while here and there pheasants scuttled for cover.

However, not all was as serene as it might have been in such surroundings. As I went along, I discovered that Braw Handsel was not about to be completely ignored by his new master, no matter what the countryside we passed through was like. He possessed several novel ways of attracting my instant attention. The most startling one of these methods involved his use of the drive chain. This would come flying off the front sprocket or chainring, and drape itself with a great clatter around the pedal crank and my foot. This happened whenever I tried to pedal too rapidly in the wrong gear, going downhill.

When I was climbing, Braw Handsel had another attention-getting trick. I would be straining uphill in the lowest possible gear, and the shift lever would suddenly come loose, shifting me into the highest possible gear, with a horrible racket from the drive chain as it bounced from the large "work" gear to the small "speed" gear. I would then find myself trying to pedal up a hill in high gear when I actually required low, and a moment later all operations would come to a halt.

The first time this happened, I thought everything was over. Then I noticed that Sun Tour was nice enough to provide a thumb screw, so I could retighten the lever and regain control over the gears. However, I still faced the problem of getting the cycle rolling uphill fast enough in high to shift back to low, as the gears only function while the chain is moving. And Braw Handsel always managed to pick fairly bad times to pull this trick on me. I decided that this act of sabotage ranked only slightly behind the thrown chain for ruining the forward flow of the day's travel.

Another quieter, but no less insidious trick that Braw Handsel offered up this first day involved the bike bags. Somehow, Braw Handsel convinced them to join him in a life of skulduggery, which they took to with enthusiasm. Like the alluring snake in the Garden of Eden, Braw Handsel whispered evil into the bike bag's flaps. As a result, they tested me always —by placing whatever I was looking for in a compartment other than the one I was looking in. As a consequence, I was forever pawing through those bags, no matter how carefully I tried to remember exactly where things were.

Finally, Braw Handsel seemed quite disturbed each time I leaned him up against a wall or pole and began to walk away. The cycle quickly learned that he could bring me back. He would wait until I was several yards away, then slowly turn his forward wheel and either fall over or slump down against the barrier. He got very good at this. With practice, he could time the operation so that I couldn't quite reach him—no matter

Braw Handsel, a "psycle" with a mind of its own.

how rapidly I came leaping back. I quickly became quite tired of having to pick Braw Handsel and the 35 pounds of dunnage I was carrying back up. But Braw Handsel seemed to enjoy the attention. He continued these tricks throughout the trip.

Braw Handsel's first testing of his powers did not take up a great deal of time on the opening leg of the trip, however. I was pleasantly surprised, when I reached the town of Peebles, to discover that I had covered, in a little over three hours, a distance equal to the longest I had ever ridden in one day—23 miles.

Beyond Peebles my route led east, running beside the River Tweed, through a town called Galashiels, to my destination for the day, Melrose. In a brilliant move I obeyed my rule about taking backroads whenever I could, and left the main road to Melrose by crossing the River Tweed and taking a small country lane that paralleled it toward my goal. Here no traffic bothered me, and the Scottish countryside seemed like a private estate created just for my pleasure. I barely could hear the hum of traffic from the road on the far side of the river, and was very glad to be away from it. One little stretch of lane ran beside a smaller stream, or "wee burn" as they are often called here, and leafless ash trees stood gaunt guard over it.

15

At another point, I found myself passing below a hillside covered with trees of a very strange, very faint yellowish-green hue. I later learned that these were larches, just budding into leaf with the advent of spring. As in a pointillistic painting, the tiny green buds combined with the tree's brown branches to produce a faint yellow color that made the entire hillside wreathed in a pale, sunlit smoke.

I was beginning to feel the effort of pedaling the heavily laden cycle, especially as my little country lane seemed inclined to bound up and down over the hills alongside the River Tweed. During this section I also discovered another rule that I tried to follow attentively throughout the trip: Never ride with your mouth open while passing by a farmyard close to the road, as you will tend to get a mouthful of flies.

Finally, my little country lane recrossed the river and joined the main route on the other side, forcing me once again to mind the speeding juggernauts. I pedaled to Galashiels, and found just enough light left to continue on to Melrose.

When I finally got off Braw Handsel (after 48½ miles), my arms ached and my rump felt as though someone had been beating on it with a two-by-four. With a bit of searching through the narrow streets of Melrose, I finally found a very nice B&B located just outside the town center. A long, hot bath there in a typically gigantic tub went a long way toward putting things right, and a "Chicken in a Basket" meal at the local pub completed the process. Then came evening tea and an enjoyable conversation with my host, and finally bed.

What with the thrown chains, slipping gear lever, missing items in the bike bags and my tired body, it hadn't been a perfect day, but it had been awfully good for a start.

Three
An Abbey, an Author,
A Loch and a Royal Visit

I awoke from a sound sleep just in time for a 9 o'clock breakfast of bread, rolls, toast, marmalade, honey, tea, eggs and bacon. Scottish B&B proprietors seem to have a hidden fear that one of their guests might starve to death at any moment, and they do everything in their power to prevent such a calamity. With unusual foresight, I took the first and last offerings of this meal and made a sandwich of them for lunch, then wolfed down all the rest.

After breakfast, I left my bike and equipment at the B&B and hurried off to wander through the remains of Melrose Abbey. Melrose dates back to the 12th century, although the ruins seen today date from only the 14th and 15th centuries. Melrose stood in the direct path of numerous English armies that invaded Scotland over various arguments, and it was demolished time after time as the English came and went. Today's remains, however, still seem awesome in their massive simplicity.

Melrose, like many ruins in Scotland, was used as a quarry for building stone for years—but enough remains to give the visitor a sense of the presence and power the abbey church must have had when whole. The south transept is especially impressive, retaining the outline of a great window, 16 feet across at the base and rising 25 feet to a gentle point. The glass is gone, of course, but the craftsmanship needed to create the window space in the stone wall is in itself evident and impressive.

The countryside surrounding the abbey is also fascinating. Directly south of Melrose the Eildon Hills lift three summits to the sky, reaching elevations between 1200 and 1385 feet. A prehistoric fort once stood on top of the north summit. Legend says that King Arthur's body lies beneath these hills, waiting to return to the world of the living. And less than two

17

miles to the east of Melrose are remains of a 1900-year-old Roman fort, Trimontium. Such ancient sites are nothing short of dumbfounding. Equally astounding is the way such sites throughout Scotland are left to themselves, with little advertising or attention devoted to them by the local people. In a way, you feel that you are discovering these places yourself—if you are lucky enough to visit them without the company of noisy crowds.

The morning haze burned off while I was at the abbey, revealing a clear, blue sky that I was to enjoy throughout the day. As I climbed aboard Braw Handsel, my sore body told me that I had traveled quite far enough the day before. However, stiffness quickly wore away as I pedaled along, making good time over the short distance to my next stop—Sir Walter Scott's home, Abbotsford.

Sir Walter Scott (1771-1832) had never loomed particularly large on my literary horizon. I could have named *Ivanhoe* as one of his works, if hard-pressed, and that would have been almost the limit of my knowledge of Scott. I was surprised then, to learn not only of the volume of Scott's creative work, but also the degree to which Scotsmen appear to revere him. In Scotland, Scott seems to be treated as the dominant figure in English literature. Many towns, at least in the area of his native Lowlands, have busts, statues or monuments to him.

James S. Stewart says, in a forward to a book on Scott: "His life and work have ennobled the Scottish scene for all time." I think this reflects the reaction of the Scots, who were defensive about their importance in the world, to a man who gave them the highest importance in all his works.

Scott's personal character also lent itself to veneration. In 1825 Scott went bankrupt through no fault of his own, yet he insisted on laboring on in the field of literature in an attempt to pay off his debts. This effort so impressed his creditors that they presented Abbotsford to him as a gift.

Abbotsford bears out the high regard Scotland held for Scott. The house contains what can only be called "relics" of the man—the last suit of clothes he wore, etc.—as well as an endless array of historical gifts (like Napoleon's pistol) given to Scott by the important men of his time. In all, Abbotsford is a shrine to a man Scotland values very highly indeed, unlike anything I have ever encountered for an American writer.

From Abbotsford, I pedaled five miles to Selkirk, a tweed milltown, and then along the River Yarrow toward St. Mary's Loch. Once again I found myself on a narrow country road. History stamped its dusty foot even on this lonely backroad, in the form of craggy Newark Castle. Built in 1423 by the fifth Earl of Douglas, Newark is a great column of stone. In 1645, General David Leslie slaughtered all his prisoners from the Battle of Philiphaugh in Newark's courtyard. (The battle was fought over the subject of religious preference between Royalists and Covenanters.) It seemed strange that such a bloody episode could have been enacted in such peaceful surroundings as those I found along the Yarrow. Yet this same juxtaposition was to prove the case time and again, throughout Scotland.

The road wound along, climbing gradually through stands of green spruce trees until it finally lifted itself to a stark, bare landscape. There were no trees here, but the rolling hillsides lay covered by an intricate brown mixture of grasses that waved in the passing breeze. I pedaled toward St. Mary's Loch, stopping only when I saw a truck dispensing bakery goods at a crossroad marked by two buildings.

Scott is said to have called St. Mary's Loch the most beautiful loch in Scotland. When I first came within sight of it, however, I felt a momentary disappointment. The loch was simply a crescent of water held in a cup of brown hills, with a single stand of trees at one end and a few more clustered along the shore. After looking for a while, though, I began to see what Scott must have meant. Just as a Mondrian painting is "just lines," so this loch was just water and surrounding hills. Nevertheless, the whole scene seemed perfectly arranged, a patch of trees here and there providing a touch of color, the combination spare and calm. And at the loch's lower end, the hills were freshly plowed in vertical furrows, appearing as though a giant's comb had neatly carved deep grooves into the rolling hillside. The road swung around the loch, and as I pedaled along I realized how quiet everything was there. Only the whisper of Braw Handsel's drive chain broke the silence.

It was becoming late, as the road led me to the boundary that separated Selkirk and Dumfries counties, high atop a pass with an altitude—enormous for Scotland—of 1100 feet. Reaching the top was work; imagine my joy at looking down the other side and seeing what appeared to be an endless downgrade through line after haze-lightened line of hills. It looked as though the road might run downhill clear to the town of Moffat, where I thought I might spend the night, and happily it did.

From the sparse surroundings of that high pass I plunged downward, at speeds that I would never have dreamed of attempting later on, passing from the bare heights to rich pastoral scenes below, flying clear to Moffat and its waiting B&B. I had covered, again to my surprise, roughly 40 miles this second day, and I felt quite comfortable in the face of that distance. And I had swallowed only one fly along the way! Just about a perfect day.

My goal for the next day was to pedal through Dumfries to a place called Glenkiln, for an audience with the King and Queen. It was warm when I left Moffat, although the haze was also far thicker than it had been during the two previous days. The backroad to Dumfries ran through a

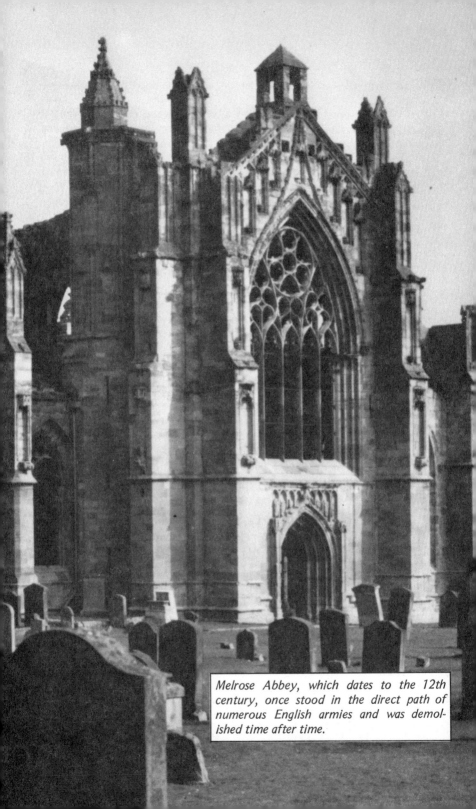

Melrose Abbey, which dates to the 12th century, once stood in the direct path of numerous English armies and was demolished time after time.

broad open valley of low rolling terrain, and as the hours passed it became warm enough to ride comfortably in just a tennis shirt.

As I went along, one of the joys of biking became evident. Cycling is such a quiet means of transportation that you can hear the birds singing along the road, sounds normally cut off if you are traveling in a car. You also move slowly enough to spot the birds in the fields. I liked the pheasants, but loved the black and white Lapwings best of all, standing like regal Egyptian pharaohs on the ground or jinking their way along in flight.

Shortly before the town of Lochmaben, and just after a pair of grouse darted from their cover directly under my path, I passed another biker, an old man working an equally old machine down the road toward town.

"Good morning," I said as I went quickly by him. "Beautiful day, isn't it?"

His entire face opened in a great smile. "Oh, aye," he said, "and tis grand indeed." Indeed. One very nice thing that I found in Scotland was the way people were always ready with a friendly greeting or a bright "Cheerio" for the passing traveler. You quickly become used to these moments of friendliness. It's a shock to visit other countries where such friendliness is not the rule, and wonder what you've done to offend everyone.

I fortified myself with an ice cream cone in Lochmaben, then pushed on for Dumfries, pedaling my way up and rushing down the slopes of the passing, rolling countryside. At one point I took a moment of rest against a comfortable moss-covered mound at a strangely lush bend of the road, the surrounding fields baking in the warm sun, as birdsong delicately wove through the trees. I couldn't help but think that the trip would be a bit of all right if it all went like this. The Scotland of rain, wind and storms that I had heard so much about seemed a myth in the face of a bright, sunny day like this.

I arrived in Dumfries early in the afternoon feeling a bit more tired than I had so far on the trip. I wondered if perhaps I wasn't pushing along too fast, goaded by the travel ethic that says, "Hurry up, hurry up, you've got a long way to go." Several soft drinks helped, however, and I took a bit of time to see two sites which, like Abbotsford for Scott, serve to enshrine another of Scotland's cultural heroes, Robert Burns (1759-1796). Like Scott, Burns celebrated the Scottish condition in his songs and poetry. He also lived a life—a rather licentious, unrestrained life—with which the common man of Scotland seemed able to identify. Burns' last home is in Dumfries, and his remains lie in a nearby cemetery.

From Dumfries the countryside became more interesting than what I had passed through in the morning. In places it was so hilly that I was forced to commit the unpardonable sin of getting off my cycle and pushing it up the steeper parts. It was simply too much work to pedal the weighted-down beast. Around me, the fields near the road were neatly rimmed with stone walls, while further away an open pasture, dotted with sheep and their snow-white lambs, swept up over the sloping land toward stands of Spruce and Larch trees capping the distant hilltops.

It was absolutely hot. I wondered how the spring lambs—there were hundreds of the little fluff-balls—could find the energy in their wool coats to carry on their fumbling, head-butting contests. It was amusing to watch them, though, as they lined up, gave each other a gentle bump, then looked surprised over having done such a thing.

I was attempting, on this jaunt, to track down a memory of something I read about years before. In an art book, I had run across a photo of Henry Moore's sculpture "The King and Queen." The description said only, "This sculpture now sits on a lonely Scottish hillside." The photo showed as powerful a piece of sculpture as I have ever seen, resplendent in its solitary location on a grassy hillside overlooking a tranquil body of water.

While I was in Edinburgh, something joggled this memory to the surface. I went into a bookstore and found a book on Moore and his work, in which the King and Queen sculpture was mentioned, but nothing was said about where the sculpture was located. Dead end. Ah, but in the back of the book, all the works were placed in their respective museums. The caption for the work I was interested in read: "The King and Queen: Glenkiln." Next, I could find no Glenkiln on the various maps I had.

On another jaunt to the bookstore I discovered a cross-reference between Glenkiln and the town of Shawhead, near Dumfries. Feeling like Holmes himself, I was determined to see this sculpture, which came to life so powerfully in those simple photographs.

In the little town of Shawhead I purchased a bottle of lemonade to slake my thirst, and asked about the royal figures. One friendly person replied, "Oh yes, the sculptures are just a wee way up yon road." Up indeed seemed the dominant characteristic, as I pedaled along for about two miles, climbing into rolling hills.

I was once again engaged in that unpardonable sin of walking the bike, when I spotted the unmistakable form of a Henry Moore sculpture off to my left, perhaps a quarter of a mile away. It was just sitting there, on a little jutting point, as if it was dropped from the sky. The Moore, a reclining "form," fronted a steep canyon with a "wee burn" at the bottom and another steep hill beyond. The sculpture, striking and well-situated as it was, was definitely not the King and Queen I sought.

At last a car came by this lonely spot, and I asked if they knew where my missing sovereigns were. The driver replied, "Oh yes, back down this road and then up that other to the reservoir." Several minutes later I found them, sitting on a green slope, overlooking a placid reservoir, with the Scottish Lowlands beyond. The gate sign said: "Private Property— Please Do Not Enter." However, the gate was unlocked and slightly ajar. After a moment of indecision, I pushed it open and ascended to the royal pair.

Moore's King and Queen are severely unadorned figures, yet they profoundly dominate the surrounding countryside. Their character seems emblematic not only of powerful royalty, but of all men and women who join together to face the world. Moore, in the turn of a shoulder, the line of a hand, has subtly caught the degree of masculinity befitting all men, the air of support and understanding that graces all women. They are a striking creation.

It was an honor to meet the King and Queen so aptly nestled on their fertile hillside with absolutely no sign, path or other man-made distraction to detract their reigning vista. (This sculpture, and several others, were placed out-of-doors here by a man named Keswick I believe, who only comes out from London for the hunting season each year. If that be his proper name or not, I would like to thank him, in any case, for providing such a perfect setting for these great figures.)

The sun was just setting into the thick evening mist as I pedaled away from Glenkiln, and the air had a cold, evening bite. I felt lucky to find a bed available in a trailer a few miles later, in the little crossroads town of Haugh of Urr. There were no tea shops in Haugh of Urr, so I dined on a nutritious supper of milk and a gooey bacon and marmalade sandwich from an earlier breakfast, followed by tea and canned tangerines. A true feast, I thought. And after all, you can't expect everything to go well on a day when you have had the privilege of meeting royalty.

Four
Threave Castle, Glen Trool And Tennis Anyone?

A fter a cold night in the trailer—the damp chill seemed extremely penetrating—I left most of my things there and rode six miles from Haugh of Urr through the town of Castle Douglas to Threave Castle. I wanted to see this castle because of a strikingly horrible event that was said to have occurred there.

Threave Castle was constructed between 1269-1390 by Sir Archibald the Grim, lord of Galloway and warden of the Western March, third earl of Douglas, whose familial line was more succinctly known as the Black Douglas:

> "Hush ye, Hush ye, little pet ye,
> Hush ye, hush ye, do not fret ye,
> The Black Douglas shall not get ye."
> English Lullaby

The Douglas family rose to prominence in the first rank of Scotland's powerful noble barons through the efforts of Sir James Douglas, known as "The Good" (1290-1330), on behalf of his king, Robert Bruce, to secure Scotland's independence from England. Sir James was a doughty and intelligent campaigner against the enemy, and he was amply rewarded with territory in southern Scotland for his efforts. When King Robert Bruce died, on June 7, 1329, his last request fell on the shoulders of the Black Douglas. Robert, never able to keep a vow that he would fight the Saracens in the Holy Land as soon as he secured his won kingdom, asked that Sir James carry his heart into battle against the Infidel. Sir James found the Infidel at Granada on August 25, 1330, but unfortunately also found his own death there as well. Even into death was the Good Sir

James faithful to his king. That compelling faith secured great lands and power to the House of Douglas.

All in the Douglas line seemed to have had a great penchant for battle against the English, who bordered on their lands. Alarmed at the vast strength of such a subject family—the House of Douglas was not only the richest in Scotland, able to put the largest number of armed men in the field, but it also had a fair claim to the throne itself—Chancellor Crichton invited the 15-year-old sixth earl of Douglas, William, and his younger brother David, to Edinburgh Castle, where they sat down to dinner in the presence of 10-year-old King James II. At the signal of a black bull's head being served, so the story goes, the two young Douglases were seized, tried and condemned of an unknown charge on the spot and beheaded. The point of this "Black Dinner" was to break the Douglas claim to the Scottish throne, and divide the Douglas wealth. This it did, but only for a time—William, eighth earl of Douglas, reunited the divided lands through an astute marriage, and once again the House of Douglas was the most powerful in the land.

Throughout the rise of the House of Douglas, the members' fortunes rested directly on their abilities as men of war, either in individual battle or as leaders of their vast hordes of feudal vassals. Douglas power and leadership was central to the defense of Scotland against incursion by the English, and often spearheaded similar incursions the other way. Naturally, this propensity for arms produced some bloody, even brutal, chapters in the Douglas family history. This warring period was more like a game for the nobles who engaged in it, however, compared to the lot of the poor peasants who made up the feudal armies of these nobles. A nobleman had a very definite value as a source of ransom, and as such was often most carefully captured and preserved. The armies of peasant vassals, on the other hand, were seen at best as targets for the exercise of lance and sword and charging horse. The English and Scottish noblemen were forever confronting one another over castle walls, then going off and burning all the surrounding towns—and townspeople—to show just how much they disliked each other.

In 1452, the eighth earl of Douglas was in a considerable state of argument with his king, as the adult James II now also saw the Douglas power as a threat to his throne. When the Black Douglas (the name was applied to the entire line) seized Sir Patrick MacLellan over some matter, and held him in the dungeon of Threave Castle, the king sent Sir Patrick Grey, MacLellan's uncle, with a royal order for the release of the Douglas prisoner. The earl insisted that he and Grey eat a proper meal before turning to matters of such importance as must be held in a letter from the king. While this meal was going on, MacLellan was taken from Threave's dungeon and beheaded in the castle yard. Douglas then opened the letter, and expressed extreme sorrow to his dinner guest that there might be some little difficulty in delivering his prisoner. Such doings on the part of a subject were, of course, perfectly designed to enrage a monarch uncertain of his hold on his own throne. This deed may have played a part in King James personally murdering the eighth earl at Stirling Castle later that same year.

There is some doubt that the murder of MacLellan actually took place in this manner—that it even took place at all—but if the murder was committed, Threave Castle certainly would have been the perfect setting for such an event. To reach the castle, I locked Braw Handsel to the fence of a small parking lot provided in the front of a nearby farmyard, then walked along a pleasant zig-zag trail that led through the farm's fields to the banks of the River Dee. From here I could see the tower of Threave Castle standing up out of encircling walls of stone, dominating the low grassy island in the middle of the Dee on which it stands. On my side of the river there was a small landing for a boat, with a large bell hanging by it. As it obviously seemed the thing to do, I rang the bell, and a few minutes later Mr. McDougal of the Commission of Works was stroking a rowboat across the river from the other side.

I was alone when I rang the bell, but by the time Mr. McDougal brought the boat in to the landing I was joined by another group: a young couple, her father and a superb golden retriever named Hector. Hector was as brave as his name might imply, of course, but he was still just a little doubtful about getting into that rowboat. As a result, it took us a few minutes to get settled in before Mr. McDougal rowed us smartly over to Threave Island and its stronghold.

From the outside, Threave Castle is very impressive in the way a stone monolith of enormous size would be. The central tower is a five-story-high stone rectangle, surrounded by a curtain wall, which originally had three-story towers at each corner. The stone of the castle is a gloomy grey, like a foreboding thunder-head, overgrown with moss—a fitting place for the Black Douglas to reside.

It is when you venture inside, however, that the full impact of Threave comes through. The central tower, 600 years old now, seems to have been built with only one thought in mind: strength! The walls are eight feet thick if they're an inch, penetrated by windows that are narrow on the outside and expand back into the rooms. As I walked into the gloom just beyond the entrance, I noticed shafts of light slanting down to the floor from two windows high overhead. It seemed I'd ventured into some place

Threave Castle is magnificent; the history of the family who created it long, intricate and macabre.

under the sea, the feeling was so heavy there. Just to the right of the entrance and along a short catwalk was a trapdoor leading down into the dungeon, and it took no imagination at all to sense how horrible it must have been for the trapped MacLellan, waiting in that tiny 10- by 14-foot box, to hear the sound of footsteps coming for him.

A spiral staircase led up to the great hall above. These stairs were common to every castle I saw, but they always amazed me every time I saw them. In each case, single stones were cut in the shape of a long, narrow pie wedge. Pile them all up in a spiral in a circular shaft, and you had a staircase that looked as though it should immediately tumble right down again, yet managed to remain standing for centuries.

Once in the great hall, you quickly realize how much art went into making these castles. Because the wooden floors are gone from the two stories overhead, and the roof as well, you see the windows and several fireplaces arranged in the walls of all three floors, hanging like strange decorations now. Each fireplace has its own chimney running up through the heavy stone to the roof, and some of the windows have what look like window seats set into the rock. No wonder this castle took 21 years to complete.

It was from this castle that the young sixth earl and his brother rode to Edinburgh and its Black Dinner, and it was also from here that the eighth earl rode to Stirling and his untimely death at the hands of his king. The eighth earl's brothers in turn rode from here to Stirling, with the king's safe-conduct that William had scorned to use, which they towed around the castle walls behind a horse, then fired the town of Stirling to show their rage at James II. The end of Threave as a Douglas castle came three years later, when Parliament formally forfeited the estates of the earl of Douglas. King James marched into Galloway to take formal submission from his lieges there, but Threave Castle, held by Margaret, countess of Douglas, the fair maid of Galloway, wife to William and then James, refused to surrender. King James immediately laid seige to the castle, but found his cannon had no effect at all on Threave's mighty walls. He then ordered a giant cannon constructed, which proved equal to the task, and Threave was surrendered by the Douglas family. The House of Douglas ceased with the ninth earl, and Threave passed into other, quieter hands.

Threave Castle is magnificent; the history of the family who created it was long, intricate and macabre. Yet there are dozens of similar castles in Scotland—possibly even hundreds—and each of them seems to hold similar tales of black deeds mixed with moments of shining heroism. What a time to live it must have been, when these castles were not ancient ruins but the grandest constructions of the day.

I spent several hours at Threave, then with the help of Mr. McDougal crossed back over the Dee, walked back through the fields to Braw Handsel and cycled back toward Haugh of Urr. On the way, pedaling hard against a headwind that had sprung up since the morning, I passed two men working on one of the stone walls lining a field by the road. The men were rhythmically plucking up stones from a stack of them, and fitting them together as fast as a card player might shuffle cards. These two would properly be called "dike men," since the stone walls they build are called "dikes." I asked one of these men just how much wall they could build in a day.

"Well, a professional dike man, now, he can build four to five yards of wall four feet high in a day," came the answer after the man thought about it a moment. "And it will last forever. But there aren't many professionals like that left today; we're just doing some repair here. It's becoming a lost art."

The man obviously enjoyed impressing me with the length of wall a good builder of walls could build in a day. But his statistics work out to something like a mile of wall in a year per man. And there must be tens of thousands of walled miles stretching over the hills throughout Scotland. All this leaves me amazed at how much can be done by mere men, moving one stone at a time, for a long, long time.

I pedaled back to Haugh of Urr, then made use of the remaining afternoon sun to take another trip, of just a mile, to a great hill that lay across the small Urr Water, and looked like a two-tiered green cake that had collapsed slightly into itself. This hill, rising abruptly from the fields that surround it, was man-made, a Saxon fortification called the Mote of Urr. It stood almost 80 feet high, and consisted of a nearly circular mound roughly 85 feet in diameter, surrounded by a ditch. The holders of such a man-made pile would have the advantage in beating off any attack mounted against them, and many places fortified with castles today began with these simple but effective strongholds. My only questions would be, how did men actually dredge up such a huge amount of earth, and how long did it take them to do it? I contemplated these matters for a long while, stretched out by the road across from the Mote, enjoying the setting sun, the green fields below me, and watching the wanderings of various rabbits and pheasants in those fileds. It had been a long, lazy day, but was very enjoyable for all that.

The next four days of travel carried me from Haugh of Urr south along the curving coastline of county Kirkcudbright (which is pronounced "Kir-COO-bree" as far as I can tell), then back north through Glen Trool and over a 1400-foot pass into the flat countryside of Ayr. For some reason

At the Whitecraigs tennis tournament, I received some prize money and the opportunity to be photographed with the John Player girls.

my energy level slipped a bit, and I found myself dawdling over any and every roadside attraction that might keep me from the work of pedaling along. The weather was warm, the air hazy in Kirkcudbright county, quite smoggy in Ayrshire, which may have added to my lethargy.

There were plenty of things to see along the way, luckily. Just a few minutes after leaving Haugh of Urr the next morning I stopped to inspect Orchardton Tower, the only round tower in Galloway, of three stories in height. Hector and his master showed up shortly after I arrived, and he made up for his hesitancy over the boat at Threave the day before by running happily around the top of the tower's stone walls, much to his owner's dismay.

Next came Dundrennan Abbey, which was built in 1142, and although it is a beautiful ruin, it looks its age, as it was used as a quarry for stone like so many other Scottish monuments.

Cardoness Castle dominated a hill just outside of the coastal town of

Gatehouse of Fleet, and sported a doorway so arranged that unwanted guests might be offered a warm welcome in boiling oil.

A bit farther on I found a much smaller castle—Carsluith—sitting happily in the middle of a private farm, looking like a misplaced brown rock among the white buildings.

There were also interesting bits of history to be learned. Robert Bruce was crowned king of Scotland at Scone on March 27, 1306, but he was forced to spend the first year of his reign fleeing the forces of King Edward I of England after losing the Battle of Methven. (Edward insisted that *he* was the feudal lord of Scotland.) Bruce and his followers were cornered by a much larger force of English at the upper end of Loch Trool, but he defeated them, and saved Scottish independence by rolling boulders down on the English from the heights above. Today the loch and its surrounding glen seem much too peaceful to have been the scene of such heated battle.

Further along, on the coast of Ayr fronting the Firth of Clyde, I passed both Crossraguel Abbey and Dunure Castle. In the 16th century, an earl of Cassillis is said to have seized the commendator of Crossraguel, Alan Stewart, and carried him off to Dunure. There the earl roasted the good Mr. Stewart over a fire, until that worthy agreed to sign over the lands of the abbey to the earl. My only question is, did Alan Stewart survive this treatment, or was he merely spared further torture before death, when he signed over the lands?

For the most part, though, I just pedaled along fitfully through this portion of the trip, accepting the countryside but not feeling terribly enthusiastic over it, especially in connection with the flat grey lands stretching between the cities of Ayr and Glasgow. I'm sure that there are some beautiful areas in Ayrshire—the guide book says they are there—but I didn't see them. Or perhaps my attention just wasn't fully centered on the country I was passing through. An adventure of another sort awaited me in Glasgow.

During the opening unit of cycling, from Edinburgh south to the Solway Firth and then back up to Glasgow, I was carrying among all my other too heavy items a tennis racket and one set of tennis clothing. By chance, my B&B in Edinburgh was located just a few doors down from the office of the Scottish Lawn Tennis Association. I had gone into the office while in Edinburgh, looking for a game of tennis and while idly glancing through a few notices there, found that Glasgow was scheduled to hold a tennis tournament just about the time that I intended to be there. When you have spent years learning, playing and teaching tennis, the sport becomes a habit as much as a conscious pursuit, and out of habit I wrote to the Whitecraigs Tennis Club to ask if I might enter their tournament. I would have liked to play at least some tennis in Scotland, and I also knew that the tournament would give me a chance to stay with a Scottish family on a more extended and personal basis than is found in the B&Bs.

Circumstances conspired to make my appearance at the Whitecraigs Tennis Club as unimpressive as possible. A few miles outside of the suburb of Glasgow where the tournament was to be held—Newton Mearns—I had my first real accident of the trip. I was traveling on a fairly narrow, quite rough road running through the fringes of Glasgow's suburbs, surrounded by increasing traffic. At one point I swung by a little old lady who was engaged in strange maneuvers to get her car around an innocuous turn, only to find her right on my tail a moment later, her front bumper nearly touching my rear wheel. The little old lady couldn't quite seem to work up the nerve to pass me—the road had a slight twist and dip to it ahead—and her companion, a much older lady, seemed to be no help. The car stayed inches from me for a nerve-wracking 100 yards, until I finally realized that this perilous situation could not proceed any longer. In desperation I decided to pull out on an open spot beside the curve ahead, near the path of two lady pedestrians. With one eye paying close attention to the car so close behind, and another heeding the path of the two lady walkers, I had none left to recognize clearly that my intended departure point from the road was covered by a nice layer of gravel.

Things proceeded quite rapidly from then on. Unable to slow my speed with the car so close behind, I left the road at a rapid pace, completing the maneuver on my side and back with Braw Handsel cartwheeling over me. The little old lady driver was quite appalled by all this, stopping her car instantly in view of my misfortune. She would have come rushing back, but I managed to hop up from under the bike and wave her away before she could. The two other ladies were equally amazed, but they also accepted my affirmation of good health and whole body.

As for me, I was sore, bleeding, absolutely filthy, minus an air pump, quite glad that nothing more had gone wrong with the bike and aware of one more item to add to my expanding rule notebook: heavily laden bicycles do not travel very well in loose gravel on a curve. I mounted Braw Handsel again, and proceeded on toward the tennis club.

As a result of all this, I entered the club looking like a reject from the garbage bin—clothes filthy and torn, blood crusted here and there. In addition, I had decided at the start of the trip not to bother with shaving, as I love any excuse to avoid that chore. My beard was now just a little over a week old, the scruffiest possible point in that enterprise as well.

In all, I wasn't too surprised when I got a number of looks of a "who's

33

that and what's *he* doing here?" nature. But everyone was of course too nice to say anything, and after I introduced myself, the people at the club immediately went to work to make me feel welcome.

It is common practice in Great Britain to house tennis tournament players in the private homes of club members. Such was the case at Whitecraigs. But never have I ever had such housing as I received there. The afternoon of my arrival, I was placed in the gargantuan hands of the club's vice-president, Alistair Campbell. Alistair is a 25-year-old Glasgow lawyer, stands a rail-thin 6 feet 7, has red hair and is possibly the funniest person I've ever met. Alistair took me to the home of his mother, Mrs. Betty Campbell, that evening, and there I remained for the rest of the tournament week and several days beyond.

Mrs. Campbell, a woman of very quiet manner, with a wit as dry and fast as a rapier, had many wonderful qualities, but one stood out to make my stay in her home pleasant beyond words. She fancied that I was on the verge of starvation, and she set herself to do the most she possibly could to prevent such a catastrophe from befalling her house guest.

I rose to a breakfast of fruit and cereal, eggs, toast and tea. If I happened to be in the house about 11 o'clock in the morning, like magic there appeared a platter of cookies and cakes and another pot of tea. Lunch might, for example, consist of soup, potatoes, herring, bread, toast, tea and some wonderful dessert such as fruit and chocolate pudding. Dinner was, of course, a feast in comparison with the earlier meals. And then, just to prevent any backsliding, there was sure to be cake and tea about 10 o'clock in the evening.

I hasten to admit that all of this did no good whatsoever for my tennis, but I also must say that it surely was enjoyable. At one point, Mrs. Campbell, speaking in short, compact sentences, as though she insisted on ridding them of all dross, voiced her opinion that "housewives should take pride in their cooking." She felt that this pride most certainly did not include using frozen, packaged foods. Amen and thank you.

I learned a great deal about Scots while staying with the Campbell family for this extended period. I learned, for example, that the Scots have a very cautious regard for electricity. For them, it is an insidious force, energizing an electrical appliance when you least expect it. As a result of this view, the normal drill for turning off such electrical appliances as a television or a floor lamp is somewhat longer than our routine. First, you turn off the appliance. Next, you flip a switch, built into the wall socket, to "off." Then, for good measure, you pull out the appliance plug as well. *That* takes care of the devilish stuff.

I also learned something about Scottish frugality with such a common item as household heat. We wantonly release heat in all the rooms of our houses, letting it pour forth into the outside world through doors and windows. The Scots carefully shelter and hoard their BTUs.

In Mrs. Campbell's home, heat was released with any real abandon in one room only—the dining room-sitting room. A fireplace and floor heater were employed with a good deal of vigor here. Elsewhere in the house, however, it was advisable to keep your parka near at hand at all times. All of which is of course the height of sensibility in this day of shorter energy rations for all. Also, such an arrangement made for excellent sleep. The bedroom might be freezing, but I would lie well-protected under down quilts in a soft bed that just begged me to stay there hours after I should have emerged back into that cold.

The word cold in Scotland reminds me of another aspect of the country that I recognized for the first time at Newton Mearns. The Scots have a different definition for toast than we do. I was brought up to believe that toast was bread that had been cooked and was still warm, so that butter would melt on it properly. The Scots, on the other hand, believe that toast is bread that has been toasted at some point in the past—20 minutes to an hour being quite acceptable. All this was just a matter of differing definition—English is not the common language between British and Americans that people say it is. As a result, I seldom received toast in Scotland despite being served toast wherever I went.

All this talk about different aspects of cold might suggest that there had been a change of weather from its state earlier in the trip, and such was the case. It drizzled the night of my arrival, and was cold and wet the next two days. I was forced to wonder if I was going to get through my trip in a completely dry condition after all. Maybe it really could rain in Scotland.

As for the tournament itself, it went very well indeed, despite its start under drizzly skies. I arrived two days before the tournament was to begin, in order to get in a bit of play before finding myself in a competitive situation. I was very rusty, it felt odd to use the running shoes I was biking in instead of tennis shoes and I had some difficulty getting used to the club's slow, hard courts. (As a Californian, when I say hard court I mean a court with a solid surface, like cement. The term in Britain or Europe would suggest a clay court.) But quickly enough I rediscovered which end of the racket was which, and I seemed to grow stronger and stronger with each early match that I played. The sun also reappeared, which helped a great deal.

It was great fun to compete against completely unknown opponents, before people who had come out to see the odd American visitor. I felt no pressure, just enjoyed hitting the tennis ball, and found myself winning fairly handily. Of course, whenever you win at something at which you used to be good, you are in effect, at least for a time, peeling back the years and returning to a more youthful condition. I don't mean to give the impression that I am ancient—I wasn't quite 30 at the time—but I can remember days when I was more adept at tennis than I am now. As soon as that happens, in terms of tennis, you are old.

In the quarters of the tournament I finally came up against an experienced player, Mr. Ken Reeve, Scotland's under-21 champ of the time. I almost snatched defeat for myself by trying too hard during the second set and consequently losing it, but with luck I captured the third and the match. In the semifinals I played a former Scottish under-21 champ, John Howie, and then faced Scotland's No.2 man in the finals, Harry Mathieson. I had seen Harry play 10 years or so earlier, when he competed on the international circuit, and it was a pleasure to face such an opponent on the warm afternoon of the finals before a friendly crowd. Still loose from my morning match with Howie, I played very well, Mr. Mathieson was slightly off, and I managed to score my first tournament win in almost five years.

I can only say winning is fun, especially after four years of either not playing tournaments, or not playing well enough to win the few I did enter. It was particularly fun at Whitecraigs. I received not only some prize money that I did not know was riding on the final, but also the opportunity to have my picture taken with my arms around the John Player Girls—two models sent out by the sponsoring cigarette company to pose with whoever won the event. It seemed that at least one of the girls felt it rather above and beyond the call of duty to pose in the grasp of such a scruffy, bearded ruffian as myself, but I enjoyed it all enormously.

The day before, Mrs. Campbell and I had entered into the best dialogue of my entire trip over my appearance.

"Now that I know you better," she began, "may I ask, is that a beard you are growing?"

"Well, yes it is," I replied. "I just don't like shaving when I am traveling."

Mrs. Campbell nodded a moment, then capped the conversation. "It is a bit in the awkward stage, isn't it?"

The next day I rode into town with Alistair, and took the train from Glasgow to Edinburgh, in order to return my tennis racket to my B&B there, and pick up my sleeping bag. I also went to Mr. MacDonald's shop for a new air pump and batter-powered night lights for the cycle.

The train back to Glasgow arrived just in time for me to enjoy another delicious meal with the Campbells. I ended my day not only stiff as a board from the previous day's play—this despite a laughable sports page statement that I was "fitter" than Harry Mathieson—but stuffed to the gunnels with delicious food besides. Thank God I didn't have to play any more matches the following day.

Five
On to Oban and Mull

The first 300 miles of the bike trip ran south from Edinburgh, through the Scottish Lowlands, then swung north through Ayr and Ayrshire to Glasgow. Now I intended to head up toward the Northwest, leaving the Lowlands for the emptier, less pastoral grandeur of the Scottish Highlands and Western Islands.

After a week playing the role of tournament tennis player, it was nice to slip back into the activity I had come to Scotland to pursue. Fortified by breakfast and two additional pieces of lemon meringue pie, I bade good-bye to Mrs. Campbell and cycled off toward the heart of Glasgow.

Today Braw Handsel seemed a bit sulky, perhaps from being incarcerated in the Campbell's coal cellar during the tennis tournament. Several times I had to pump more air into the cycle's tires, and one of Braw Handsel's handbrakes also was loose. In addition, the brakes would freeze in a closed position, instead of snapping back open when released. A visit to Glasgow's largest bike shop—Rattrays—seemed essential before heading north. As ignorant as I was about cycling in Scotland, I did know there were few bike shops north of the Glasgow-Edinburgh line. (I did not know that I would be searching out most of them before the trip was over.)

The traffic in Glasgow was terrifying to deal with. I also very quickly became out of sorts with Glasgow's streets, which were all torn up or blocked by construction or not in their mapped locations. I soon realized that finding this particular bike shop was like seeking the exit of an endless maze, but at last Braw Handsel and I managed to thread our way through.

Once at Rattrays, a very quick and silent repairman yanked my brake cable out of its sleeve, oiled it, put it back again and tightened it, spilling no more than a tablespoon or so of oil all over my bike bags in the process.

Next I had to get back out of Glasgow. At first it was again like riding through a maze. Then, as the miles rolled by, the city buildings turned to village shops, and finally I found myself back in the quiet country running beside the Firth of Clyde, the heavy industrial and shipping sections of Glasgow thankfully behind me. The air was very hazy, as usual, cutting down my visibility considerably.

I reached the small, neat country town of Balloch, at the lower end of Loch Lomond, late that afternoon. At this point, I could not decide if I should turn left and head directly toward the West Coast, or swing right, toward Loch Lomond's east shore and on to the area called the Trossachs. This indecision gave me an excellent excuse to stop at a hotel tea room to review my maps over a bacon omelet. Finally, I decided to head west, hoping to see the Trossachs (often termed the entrance to the true Highlands) on the way back.

After a short distance I was startled by a number of large bears gamboling on a green field under spreading trees. Bears in Scotland? Yes, in this case, behind the fences of the Lomond Bear Park. I walked along the fence, enjoying the sights for free, spellbound by these frolicking bears living in such a large enclosure, instead of listlessly confined to tiny zoo cages or rock gardens.

At last I pedaled on up the mist-concealed shores of Loch Lomond, until dark finally caught me. I spent that night in a small, very neat cottage by the lake's shore, sharing the hospitality there with another couple from South Africa. The next morning I was up early, for the usual large breakfast, then set off on my way again.

Thanks to the ubiquitous haze I never did get a really good view of Loch Lomond. Still, a sweep of shore and an island floating in the mist did suggest some of the visual beauty that has made Loch Lomond so famous. The countryside was rougher and steeper than in the South. I was amazed at how barren Loch Lomond is of buildings and housing developments, considering what a famous place this is, and how close it lies to the population of Glasgow. But that is one of the great charms of Scotland—the way it has remained so undeveloped, at least to an American's eyes, with its cities tightly contained and its countryside left untouched.

Loch Lomond's history carried a different note from any I had read about in the South. The MacGregors and the Colquhouns were the principal clans on the loch, and they naturally fought each other tooth and nail, of course. But in 1263 another element intruded on Loch Lomond that must have been a shock to both clans. The viking Magnus dragged his ships across the two-mile ridge of land separating Lomond from the sea, and fought *his* way up and down the loch. Think of the inhabitants, sitting by the shore of a land-locked lake, planning the next raid on their neighbors, and then having a Viking ship come racing at them out of the gloom. Those were truly unsettled times.

Pedaling along, up the west side of Lomond, across to Loch Long, then up to an 880-foot pass named "Rest and Be Thankful," I realized that I was still gun-shy from my fall the previous week. I was unwilling to go down hills with anywhere near the speed I used before. In addition, I viewed all gravel anywhere near the road as a mortal enemy, undoubtedly plotting another fall for me. Apparently, the sense of invulnerable well-being that had encompassed me for the first miles of the trip was stripped away by the fall outside of Glasgow. I could get hurt, after all. To make matters worse, the drive chain threw twice during this day's travel. Naturally, this always happened when I needed to make some quick move. My problem was just a drive chain with one or two links too many. Nevertheless, it seemed as though Braw Handsel had something to do with the awkward timing of these occurances. Such events couldn't have happened, with such painful timing, without the guidance of some malicious spirit.

I also realized, pedaling along, that I was growing tired of spending quite so much money for lodging. This evening, I decided, I would economize—in fact, I would spend nothing—by camping out under the stars. Of course, I couldn't see stars, or anything else, from the ridge above Loch Awe where I decided to stop. Cold, heavy fog had come rolling over the hill with the setting sun. But what did that matter, in the face of such an economic triumph? I spread out my sleeping bag, munched a dinner of scones and yogurt, and slid off to sleep, still pleased with my bargain.

By three the next morning I knew that I had been "penny wise and pound foolish." By then, the water-filled mist had dumped enough liquid to soak clear through my down bag, turning it to a damp, clinging shroud with the insulating power of an ice cube. Earlier, I poked my head out to discover that my air pillow was sopping wet. Now it was nicely frozen, rock hard. I struggled in the bag, putting on my short and long sleeved shirts, a tracksuit top, long pants and a parka hood, and managed to get back to sleep until the first grey light of dawn woke me again.

It was much too cold to stay where I was, so I struggled up and packed all my sopping gear into the sopping bags on sopping Braw Handsel.

I rode downhill to Loch Awe, and spotted Kilchurn Castle. It looked interesting, a black fist of power in the swirling mist, but the thought of a warm cafe in the nearby town of Dalmally was much more alluring. Unfortunately, I was experiencing this anticipation around six in the morning, and Dalmally's single cafe didn't open before nine. I spent the time in the waiting room of the town's tiny train station, trying to get some warmth back into my hands and feet. When the cafe finally opened, the tea, toast and eggs I consumed next to a blazing floor heater soon made a marked improvement in my condition.

At last, having absorbed as much warmth from the cafe as I could, I mounted up and rode down the long arm of Loch Awe leading to the Pass of Brander. After a mile or two I was startled to realize I was passing the lower end of the world's second largest hydro-electric power station of the sort where water is pumped to a higher reservoir and then allowed to drop back to produce power. All I could see was a tree-covered slope, and an attractive low building on Loch Awe itself. There was no sign at all of disturbance on the mountainside, no hint of the great water tubes and underground access road buried there. (In contrast, American engineers seem to believe it necessary to clear a 200-yard swath around any sort of industrial operation before even beginning.) What a pleasant sight this was.

From the Pass of Brander, where King Robert Bruce nearly destroyed the clan of MacDougall of Lorn in 1308, I glided down a sloping road into the town of Taynuit, stopped for lunch and then rode on beside Loch Etive and Dunstaffnage Castle to the town of Oban.

Oban is a pleasing harbor town on the Firth of Lorn, its small but secure harbor packed with fishing vessels and the large car ferries that carry people to the nearby island of Mull. I thought that I would catch one of these ferries this evening, but on inquiry I learned that I had missed the last. I was not too unhappy, however, as I felt extremely tired from lack of sleep and the long day's efforts. It took only a few minutes to ride back through town, to a B&B I had spotted on the way in.

A pleasant proprietoress at the B&B assured me that a room was available and that I could carry my cycle upstairs if I wished. This was quite a feat, considering the narrow stairs and the tiny room that Braw Handsel half-filled. But I found it easier to handle the cycle this way each night if I could, rather than unloading it. I also slept better, knowing that my means of transport was safe beside me, instead of wondering what might be happening to it outside.

I left Oban the next morning, taking the car ferry to Craignure on the island of Mull. Before our departure, all passengers on the ferry were treated to an unplanned but first-class comedy act. Five men were attempting to drive three black bulls onto the ferry, but the bulls wanted no part of it. As a result, time and again the stubborn animals ran like quicksilver through the line of five men who were trying to drive them aboard. One man in particular seemed destined to ruin the efforts of the other four. Each time they managed to get two of the bulls to stand still, this fifth man felt the urge to punish them with a great whack of his stick, which

Oban is a pleasing harbor town on the Firth of Lorn, its small but secure harbor packed with fishing vessels and the large car ferries that carry people to the nearby island of Mull.

instantly sent them off in seven different directions, none of which involved the ship. This went on for a good 20 minutes, luring everyone on board to the ship's railing and everyone on the dock below to watch the comedy.

Finally, the bulls and all the rest of the passengers and cargo were all herded aboard, and the ferry steamed out of Oban's harbor. On our right, one of the most beautiful castle ruins in Scotland looked down on us from a little hill. All that remains of Dunollie Castle is a single tower of rock clasped tightly by great vines of ivy, but it still dominates the harbor it has guarded for seven or eight centuries.

Ahead, heavy mist floated over the Firth of Lorn, and even after landing, Mull, called the Mountainous, might have been better named Mysterious Misty Mull for all that I could see.

From the landing point at Craignure, on Mull's eastern side, I planned to cycle northwest along the island's coast toward Mull's major town, Tobermory. I had not pedaled far before I discovered that travel on Mull can offer plenty of adventure. The roads there proved to be only one lane wide, with pull-out spots provided every few hundred yards. All cars, trucks and buses on the road of course ignored something as puny as a lone cyclist, so I quickly learned that it payed to plan each advance, leaping from pull-out to pull-out before being run off the road.

Just outside the little town of Salen, I spotted my first Highland bull. These are super beasts, huge and red in color, with a fringe of hair hanging down over their eyes, giving them an extremely "hippy" look.

I passed through Salen, thinking that I needed something to eat, but still not quite stopping. A little farther along I spotted a sign at a farm inviting the traveler to come in, not only to see home-made pottery, but to sample some home-made fudge as well. This I couldn't pass up, so I walked Braw Handsel over the rough path to the farmhouse.

A heavyset man made me welcome to a little shop stuck onto the main farmhouse, where he and his family sold their artistic output. He specialized in the fudge—one *ton* of it was sold the previous year—while the rest of his family worked along more normal artistic lines. The room held some very fine watercolors, set alongside some poor oils and horrid ceramics.

I purchased only a handful of fudge, but this did not seem to disturb the proprietor. He happened to mention that he had sold 1000 acres to a private tree farmer just the year before, so I guess the little store was more hobby than necessity.

Tree farming is a major business throughout Scotland. The trees, when properly grown, are one of the few things that can compete with the thick peat so common to the Scottish Highlands and islands. My fudgeman de-

Highland bulls are super beasts with hair that gives them a "hippy" look.

scribed how the trees were grown, which also explained the great furrows I had seen at the start of the trip in such places as St. Mary's Loch and the Glen Trool Forest. The trees cannot grow directly in peat, so giant plows turn deep grooves of it out of the ground to dry in the sun. After a year or two the trees are planted on top of this pile, and the open ditches are used for irrigation. These gigantic tree farms are changing the appearance of much of Scotland, but historically Scotland was far more a land of forests than it is today. The trees disappeared several hundred years ago, burned for charcoal or cleared for sheep pasturage.

Munching my fudge, I pedaled toward Tobermory. The air, opaque with mist, was so cold that a simple pair of gloves became a welcomed comfort. I might add how surprised I was to discover the marked change in temperature I felt after putting a pair of gloves on, or a knit cap. With some experience, these items became my main means of changing my body temperature, rather than more complicated changing of shirts, parkas and windbreakers.

Going from Oban to Tobermory is like going back in time some 50 or 100 years. Tobermory, 1/10 the size of Oban, on Mull's upper tip, lies snugly about a small, protected harbor. Its tranquil setting suggests a town of a different era nestled in the tiny bay. As quiet as the town appeared to be, it had its exciting moment in history. A ship from the Spanish Armada was blown apart in its bay in 1588, by a Scotsman disgruntled at being held prisoner aboard her.

Braw Handsel and I snaked along through the small town's upper streets, making our way down to the waterfront and its perfect line of small shops and buildings. One of these, I was told by a battered copy of the Scottish Youth Hostel Association (SYHA) booklet I had found in Edinburgh, was a grade three (no showers, cold tap water, etc.) youth hostel of 42 beds with a small store.

At this point I was not a member of the SYHA. But lodging expenses of the last several nights combined with my single miserable attempt at sleeping out greatly increased my interest in joining. Youth hostels in Scotland charge less than a dollar for a night's lodging. For this fee you get a warm place to spread out a sleeping bag, and access to a kitchen area where you're free to cook whatever you desire. Often, the hostels include a small store.

There are 80 of these marvelous hostels scattered about Scotland, and they have to be the best bargain around. Unless, I discovered, you are an American trying to join. In this case, where a Scotsman would be charged only 75p (about $1.80), an American must pay almost $10. This is because the American Youth Hostel Association charges so much for membership in our limited chain of hostels that other national associations feel they must return the favor.

I learned all this from an energetic, white-haired lady who, with her husband, ran the Tobermory hostel. At $10 to join it took me several minutes of wrestling with myself before I handed over the required funds. I received a pink temporary membership slip in return, and after taking a look at it I handed it back to the woman. She would hold it through the night, and return it only after I had done, to her satisfaction, whatever job of cleaning she assigned the next day. Through these chores, which every hosteler does before leaving, the buildings of the system remain spic and span at minimum expense.

There was only one other person in my room of eight bunks, a most acceptable ratio. I was lucky this way almost throughout the trip. I often had to share quarters with only one or two other people, or with no one at all. On this basis, a hostel dorm is very nice. When they are jammed, as they are during the summer, they are much less comfortable.

After arranging my bunk I hurried back downstairs, to whip up the dinner of packaged curry and rice I purchased from the hostel store. In the small kitchen I found a set of shelves with cups, plates, pots, pans and teakettles, a row of gas burners, three girls and my roommate. Very quickly, I found myself included in their conversation.

46

This is another nice aspect of the hostels—each night you are assured of finding interesting people, who more than likely have been doing activities similar to your own. Fellow guests always want to talk over events of the day, or their plans for the next, producing a ready sense of community at any hostel. The man with whom I was sharing the men's bunk room was spending his holidays walking over this rugged Scottish island, trying to avoid roads and trails as much as possible. Two of the girls were randomly hitchhiking in whatever direction fate carried them. The third had attended the University of California at Santa Barbara, lived in Jamaica, crewed a trans-Atlantic boat race and was working in London as a nurse before going on to India.

Everywhere the hostels lodged young adventurers like these. Some of them, particularly those from New Zealand and Australia, pursued amazing five-year plans of travel and work through Europe. With such company as this, the hostels are a nice change from a steady diet of B&B living.

The interesting spellbinder of the evening, however, was the husband of the woman who ran the hostel. He was a rail-thin man, perhaps 55 or 60 years of age, with a superb, instant laugh and a wonderfully rolling way with words. His thick Scottish accent was a delight to listen to, his observations very interesting as well.

What started him off escapes me. Perhaps I used the word "British" when I should have said "Scottish." However, after warming himself by the old-fashioned iron stove, the old gentleman began to explain why the Scots have such a deep feeling of nationalism for such a small country. (As is so often the case with individuals, the points of conflict did not center on wide national concerns that would seem important, but more on the little things that get under a person's skin.)

At one point he explained, "When you watch a sports program, whenever the winner is English he is called English, but if the winner is Scottish he is called British. But turn it around, and if the loser is Scottish, he is always named as such, while the Englisher gets away with being named British." Later, warming to his speech, he said, "They sing in England of never being conquered. Well, the Romans make us the only ones who can sing that song."

He also talked a bit about Mull and life on the island: "The people here just want to be left alone. They don't like change. They're against the Forestry Commission, because it owns so much of the land here. Another problem is how hard it is to find homes here today. They are too expensive to build, as all the materials have to come from the mainland, and so many rich English have bought second homes here that they drive the price out of reach of any of the people already living here."

47

But there were compensations, the old gentleman admitted, for anyone who moved to Mull and stayed in one of its tiny communities.

"No one dies of ulcers here," he said. "And here, they din'a work to the clock, they work to the calendar. It's a nice place for home to be."

The six of us talked on into the night, well past the normal 11 o'clock lights out. But finally we all agreed that it was time for bed, and the warm circle around the stove broke up at last.

I was blasted awake by the town's nearby bell early the next morning. After breakfast the other hostelers and I walked around, looking into the shops that shouldn't have been open (Britain sets the hours that shops may be open) but were anyway. Later, I packed Braw Handsel and wheeled him out to the street. My roommate, Ben, asked if he might try the cycle. As he pedaled cautiously away from me I wondered briefly if the rear wheel wasn't somehow out of line—it looked as though it had a wobble to it. But of course nothing could possibly go seriously wrong with such a bike as Braw Handsel. So I ignored the wobble I was seeing, and set off on my longest day of cycling to date—a winding 65 miles around the west coast of Mull—from Tobermory to Bunessan.

I decided to circle Mull for a number of reasons, but on this day each was thwarted. I wanted to catch a glimpse of three unusually-named islands—Rum, Eigg and most particularly Muck. But the cursed haze filled the air as usual and completely concealed these islands that lie just to the north of Mull. I also had hope of taking a ferry from Ulva to the island of Staffa, a geological curiosity off the west coast of Mull, but the Ulva ferry proved to be in Oban for repair. Finally, I wanted to see as much of Mull as possible, but again the haze interfered. As I pedaled along, all these negative results seemed to drain me of energy.

But then I began to discover compensations in this day, despite the haze. Passing by a field beside the road, I stopped to watch a beautiful new-born colt prancing and gamboling on rickety-strong legs all about its patient mother. Further on, at the head of Loch na Keal, four English bikers invited me to join them for a cup of coffee, and I offered a broken bit of mint cake to the feast. These four had traveled with me on the ferry from Oban. They were heavily weighted down, carrying pots, pans and a gallon of wine in their baskets, bags and backpacks. The four way-farers were obviously having a lark, despite the cold misty afternoon that kept us huddling down among some rocks by the shore, out of the wind.

Before leaving these four, I helped them to pump up their tires, as they had no pump with them. I was surprised to notice something about my own bike as well: I had a broken spoke in the rear wheel. Astonishingly, I filed this bit of information in my mind's circular file, along with the morning's item of the wobbly wheel. I mean, what could one little broken spoke matter when there were so many of them left in the wheel? Anyway, I had heard that there was a bike shop in Oban. I would have the spoke fixed there.

After I left my fellow bikers, a vagrant breeze blew some of the mist aside at last, providing my first glimpse of one of the peaks that make Mull worthy of the sobriquet, "Mountainous." I was seeing the foot and lower slopes of Ben Moore, a Scottish giant at 3185 feet. Suddenly the day didn't seem so bad after all.

I felt much better for my visit with other bikers, and the bit of food we had together. I was heading for the town of Bunessan, 33 miles away at the opposite end of Mull from Tobermory, but now I felt energized, with much more interest in my surroundings. A field at the head of Loch na Keal held several stages, one of which was pure white. Further on I had a brief conversation with a herd of cows and calves happily chewing their cud. A little farther along, the road ran right down to the rocky shore, forced there by high green cliffs that looked like Hawaiian pali. The setting sun turned the calm ocean to gold.

It was a long climb up and across the point of land dividing Loch na Keal from Loch Scridain. The effort was rewarded, however, by a long, straight two-mile downhill run to Loch Scridain in the last minutes of daylight.

Breathless from the speed and cold, I stopped to put my battery-powered head and taillights on Braw Handsel and my parka on me and pedaled on. My fatigue increased as I failed to find a place to stop for the night. (About now I also noticed that my rear wheel seemed to be rubbing gently against the frame.) Finally, a little after 10 o'clock, I stumbled into the bar of Bunessan's one hotel, and asked the bartender if any rooms were available. He was shocked that anyone could ask anything of him after hours. He retorted, "Don't you know it's after 10, lad?" This provoked a sharp reaction from me, as I explained to him that the hour had little to do with my needing a bed and rest. Luckily, as I stalked out of the bar, a couple who were leaving caught up with me and offered the comfort of their home.

Their place was rather strange for Scotland, all crisp and new, plastic flowers about, like something you would order out of a Blue Chip catalogue. Perhaps it was the result of some sort of government project. And in a way, my host did work for the government. He was one of the men who ran the official ferry from Mull to Iona that I planned to take the following morning.

The couple was kind enough to give me a sandwich to eat and tea to drink, and directly afterward I went upstairs to bed and sleep. As I dozed off, I wondered about the rear wheel somehow shifting so that it would rub against the frame. It wasn't much—I had finally fixed it by readjusting the wheel—but it seemed an irritation I didn't need. Little did I realize, as I lay there, just how much irritation Braw Handsel was to supply over the next several days.

Six
Iona, Staffa and Braw
Handsel Goes on Strike

Ross: Where is Duncan's body?
MacDuff: Carried to the Colme-kill,
The sacred storehouse of his predecessors,
And guardian of their bones.

Shakespeare, *Macbeth*

No one knows whether or not MacBeth killed Duncan in the manner Shakespeare describes, but Duncan's last resting place, "Colme-kill," is known. It is the island of Iona, nearly a mile off Mull's western shore. A.D. 563, Saint Columba of Ireland came to this low, lonely island, and brought with him the first whisperings of Christianity to stir in Scotland. He worked to convert Scotland's Northern Picts, and in the end managed to spread the word of his God as far as Iceland.

It was hard to believe, standing at the lonely end of Mull, looking across the narrow channel toward Iona, that this remarkably remote spot was once "the unquestioned center of Christian teaching in Europe." Iona was such an important spot that it drew not only living men of religion, but the bodies of Scottish, French, Irish and Norse Kings as well. It is hard, for me at least, to picture so much history happening in such a small, quiet corner of the world.

To give some idea of how remote this area of the world is, it took me a little over an hour to cash a traveler's check. One of the two storekeepers insisted on phoning a bank on the mainland to learn the proper rate of exchange, despite my willingness to cash the blasted thing at almost any rate he cared for. Finally the lengthy transaction was very properly completed, and I rode off on my way to Fionnphort and the Iona ferry.

51

I just missed the ferry by a minute as it pulled away on its mile crossing. So I waved to my host of the night before who was navigating, and settled down to wait. It was actually a pleasure to spend some time on the Mull side of the run. The ferry docked in a rocky little bay with very clear water and colors straight out of a Dali seascape.

Once on Iona, I decided that the island holds more fascination in its historical connotations than in what remains there today. St. Mary's Cathedral seemed positively recent, dating as it does from the 16th century, and all the rest of the island struck me as somber and grey. I did like the 14-foot high granite shaft called St. Martin's Cross, which stands just outside the cathedral. It was sharply carved with Runic drawings and figures, and dates from the 10th century.

After waiting for the ferrymen to finish lunch, I crossed back to Mull. In the ferry parking lots I made use of one of the bright red phone booths that dot all of Great Britain—I've heard it said you are always within a mile or so of one wherever you are—to call a man I'd been told could take me to the island of Staffa.

Alan Logan came on the line, sounding very bright and pleasant, and said that yes, he would certainly take me to Staffa. He had to point out, though, that he normally received six pounds sterling each time he took his boat out, and that he would have to charge me that amount even if I were the only passenger. I gulped and said that I would have to think it over, that I would try to find someone else who might care to go along, and that I would phone him back from Bunessan. He said fine, pointed out that it was a lovely day, perfect for going to Staffa, and said good-bye.

I pedaled slowly back to Bunessan, wondering if I could afford such an expensive trip to see Fingal's Cave. It might be the chance of a lifetime etc., etc., but six pounds seemed quite steep.

At this moment, Braw Handsel began to act up. It was difficult to pinpoint, but the cycle felt funny under me, vibrating somehow as I went along. The rear wheel also began to rub against the frame again, and I had to stop once to straighten it out. Then, just as we came around a turn in view of Bunessan, I thought I heard a chunking, pinging sound nearby, but I couldn't think what it might be.

I phoned Alan Logan again, and said that yes, I would like to go to Staffa, and despite being totally unable to afford his hire I would do it anyway. "Just turn left beyond the town and follow the telephone line," he directed. "You can't miss the house, it's the last one down by a little cove around the point."

I rode the bike to the turnoff, down the far side of the cove that has Bunessan at its head, and then up a brief hill to reach the other side of

St. Martin's Cross, on the island of Iona, stands 14 feet high and dates from the 10th century.

the point. As I approached still another phone box, Braw Handsel's rear wheel suddenly began to scrape the frame again, very hard this time. I got off and used my single tool, the multi-sized nut wrench, to loosen the wheel and pull it straight. I got back on, but now the wheel was scraping on the other side. I tried again. Still scraping. Wow. My transport was simply not working. Looking ahead to the phone box, I decided that I had better cancel the trip to Staffa and concentrate on fixing the cycle. But how to do that? And what if it simply was to stop functioning, as it seemed to have every intention of doing? Suddenly, despite the warm afternoon sun and the neat houses of Bunessan on the waterfront behind me, Mull seemed like a very deserted, lonely spot in which to have a sick bike.

"You're canceling," a woman's voice stated rather than asked when I told her who I was. Then Mr. Logan came on the line—it was his sister who had answered—and asked from where I was phoning.

"But that's only 100 yards away," he protested when I told him. "Come on down, I've got tools."

As I was sorry to be canceling the boat rental in the first place, I found it difficult to refuse his command. And by obeying, I thought that Mr. Logan would see my difficulty and understand the cancellation.

Alan Logan proved to be a short, active man of middle age, with very curly hair and a twinkling eye. He was dressed in coveralls over warm pants and a heavy knit sweater, and he waved hello to me as I came into his yard. He looked very much in place in front of the low crofter's house that he, his sister and their bed-ridden mother inhabited. (A "croft" is a small holding, often with common grazing rights existing among a number of them. Croft houses were usually small, comfortable, but roughly made.)

I waved back, got off Braw Handsel, and for the first time really took a look at that rear wheel. Would you believe eight broken spokes?

It is always embarrasing to have one's stupidity thrust forcibly before one's eyes. The embarrassment is compounded when a friendly stranger is standing right there beside you when it happens. I covered my chagrin by standing up again and saying rather bruskly, "Well, let's go to Staffa. I need something to take my mind off of this."

Of course, those of you who have done any cycling knew what sort of trouble was in store for me as soon as I mentioned spotting a broken spoke on the rear wheel. It never really occurred to me that bicycles might actually break down, lose spokes or even have a flat tire here and there. These things had never happened to me before with a bike. Outside of that multi-purpose wrench and the small patch kit, I left Edinburgh with nothing—repeat, zilch—in the way of repair equipment, not even a spare inner tube.

Looking back, all this seems to be a quite stunning degree of innocence to me. Yet at the time, all anticipation of problems simply did not enter my mind. I had never been around a breaking spoke before, either, and received no message from that "chunk-pinngg" sound that I had heard coming into Bunessan—the sound of a spoke head breaking and flying off like a bullet. I can understand how irritated Braw Handsel must have become in the face of such unthinking treatment. I only wish Braw Handsel had spoken up in clear protest, instead of beginning a campaign of revenge, cunningly enacted throughout the remainder of the trip. Alan made me feel slightly better by suggesting he knew of a man who might be able to give me a ride back to the ferry for Oban in his truck. Then he invited me to come into his home. There I met his sister, his mother (who surveyed all that went on from her tiny bedroom, confined there by a slipped disk) and various assorted household pets including two sheep that poked their heads in the door. We had tea while preparing for the journey. Then Alan and I set out for Staffa and Fingal's Cave.

We walked down from the house to the low waters of the little cove, then skirted around to where a small open boat was anchored in deeper water. Alan deftly threw a boathook on a line over its gunnel, and pulled blue "Maggie Ann" within reach. We scrambled in, Alan started her up and we chugged out of the little harbor for the eight-mile ride to Staffa.

Alan, his curly hair blowing in the wind and eyes sparkling with pleasure, settled comfortably in the rear of the little boat. He proceeded to tell me of the time he missed the island completely with a boatload of visitors, and was stopped from going on to Iceland only by the helpful suggestion of a passing ship. The sun was out over us, but as usual the day was hazy. I began to hope that Staffa was a large and easily visible sort of destination.

The island of Staffa is tiny and uninhabited, with a shoreline of perhaps one-and-a-half miles. It has no buildings, no significant events have happened there and, in fact, it was only discovered in 1774. What Staffa does offer the visitor is one of the most curious geological phenomenon in the world. The island is composed of basalt, which, on cooling after the island's violent volcanic birth, formed into prismatic columns. From a distance these columns seem to support an unformed upper crust of rock and topsoil. (The island looks much the way a frosted cake might look if placed on a bed of upright toothpicks.) If the visitor is lucky enough to get ashore, he will find himself walking on a broad, sloping causeway of columns that seem to have been snipped off for the purpose.

Just offshore lies another little island, made up of fantastically twisted columns. At the end of the causeway the visitor will find Fingal's Cave, the largest of several such caverns extending into Staffa's base. Here another geological caprice of nature has punched a hole into the basalt columns. The hole is shaped roughly like a narrow shoe box, 227 feet long and 66 feet from the ocean's surface to the roof, with a like depth of ocean hiding the bottom at mean tide. Everything here, including the roof overhead, is made of those black prism-shaped pillars, looking like so many barrel-sized poles bundled together.

Because we were alone, and I was paying such an absurd amount for the trip, Alan decided to land me despite the swells that were breaking against Staffa's strange flanks. He was apologetic about it. But, because of the surf and changing tide, Alan said he could allow me only 20 minutes to examine the island. It would have been nice to spend 20 days in that strange place, but 20 minutes was enough to give me an idea of what Staffa was all about.

Alan Logan deftly steered the small boat to Staffa, an island that is a most curious geological phenomenon and the location of Fingal's Cave.

I climbed up from where Alan worked to hold the boat against a small and precarious landing spot, and marveled how the uneven tops of the basalt columns were like so many sawn tree-rounds set down for walking. I hurried along the causeway, wondering if many other people had found themselves slipping and slithering on the slick surface there, toward the waiting waves, since I was putting on just such a performance.

Around the corner was Fingal's Cave, perhaps the strangest place I have ever entered. It has a unique interior, what with the nearly mathematical precision of its components, and to this was added the working, crashing ocean floor. The whole was impressive beyond belief. I could easily understand how such a spot had served as inspiration for Mendelssohn's "Hebrides" overture. It inspired me to stand there, singing and shouting out nonsense to the ocean's boom, for as many minutes as I could spare of the 20.

A strange place, Fingal's Cave excited a feeling of power, like several other places I was to encounter on the trip. The truly unique thing about this spot, though, was that it stood as an ode to nature's infinite power and complexity, rather than to man's. I only wish that I might have camped on the island for two or three days, to watch the tides change the shape and sound of the cavern. It was an incredible place to be.

My time was up, so I hurried back along the causeway and into the boat. Alan was having a bit more difficulty controlling it now, and it took us a number of minutes to catch the right combination of incoming waves to get clear of the island. The hour-and-a-half ride back was as enjoyable as the one coming out, first watching Staffa recede into the haze, then watching the rocky coast of Mull emerge from it. As we went, I asked Alan if he had always lived on Mull.

"No," he answered with a straight face, then grinned and added, "just for the last 42 years. Tha mi nam a meiullach a 'nis," he added, I think. "I'm a Mull Man now." Alan went on to say that to be a complete member of a country community in Scotland, you have to be born into it. Otherwise, you will always be reckoned an outsider, no matter how long you live there. This seemed strange to me, coming as I do from the world's most mobile society, where a person who lives in the same spot for five years is often considered an old-time resident.

The small cove in front of Alan's home had filled with the rising tide, so he anchored "Maggie Ann" directly in front of the house and we scrambled off the prow. Inside, we had tea again, and bread and cheese. (I think Alan still felt apologetic for having to charge so much for the trip to Staffa.) Then he gave me directions to the house of the man he thought might be able to transport me back to the Craignure Ferry the following day.

The hill over which the road dropped down into Bunessan had seemed gentle and short when I first rode into town. Now it seemed steep and endless as I pushed Braw Handsel back up it. I found the man I was looking for, in a small trailer across from the local school at the top of the hill. He was very silent and dour, heard out my tale of woe, then grunted in reply that I should be ready to go at 7 o'clock the next morning and slammed the door in my face.

I walked across to the school yard, forced by events to spend my second night out in the open. I can only report that Scotland was at least quite consistent. The dew once again was truly remarkable in its ability to penetrate my down bag, and the temperature again went below freezing. In all, this second attempt at camping out was just as unsuccessful as the first.

One benefit of the miserable night, however, was that I was definitely ready to go at 7 o'clock. At last the sun came up, there was some activity in the little caravan, and finally we were off for the ride to the ferry.

My benefactor drove in deadly silence, perhaps ashamed to be seen carrying such a crazy person as a mainlander with a bicycle crammed into the back of his little van. He had to pick up several of his mates, who were working on a construction project with him. For the most part each of these gentlemen managed to show no sign of any sort that I was there. It was an amazing performance of concentrated, iron-willed indifference, and I began to understand how hard it must be for an outsider to break into such a closed society. When any words were spoken, they were in Gaelic, and served only to increase my sense of isolation.

At last the ride was over. The silent driver let me off at the ferry without a word, despite my profuse and quite heartfelt thanks. The large car-ferry from Oban was beautiful as it came drifting into the dock in the early morning sun, particularly as it represented a solution for all my problems. All I had to do was get to Oban, and the bike shop there would have me on my way in no time.

Or so I thought. As it turned out, however, there was a little problem with repairing the broken spokes on the cycle's rear wheel. The broken spokes were all located on the right side of the wheel, against the gear block, which had to come off if the spokes were to be replaced. This is done quite easily, with a neat, machine-tooled nut with two little nubbins that slip right into two little holes on the block, allowing the gear block to be twisted loose with any large wrench. But guess what? The Oban bike shop didn't happen to have one of these nuts at the moment. And without it, the young repairman found that he couldn't budge the gear block at all—no matter how hard he tried with a pair of pliers, or banged away at it with a hammer and chisel of all things.

Suddenly, rescue did not lie in Oban, but at the end of a fairly long and expensive train ride back to Glasgow and Rattrays. Of course, Braw Handsel was just a bike, an inanimate object, but at this point I swear I could hear a muttered, "This will teach you to mistreat a Carlton Grand Prix."

I felt the pinch of spending too much money when the train ticket to Glasgow proved to cost nearly $6. Obviously, this was a huge bargain for the distance covered, but I still resented it. I was on an open-ended sort of trip, and I felt that every unexpected expense served to shorten it. One part of my mind did point out, however, that as far as keeping the cycle in repair, *any* expense was acceptable.

I bought the ticket for the next day, then spent the rest of this day try-ing to decide if I were enraged or overjoyed at this forced halt. For the first time in Scotland, the day was *clear*. There was no haze or mist anywhere, and I could see all the mountains of Mountainous Mull, as well as Scotland's highest mountains, far to the north. It was spectacular. I hated the thought of wasting a day riding the train to Glasgow, but because of this pause in the trip, I was able to enjoy my surroundings in complete leisure, with no sense of having to hurry on.

The next day I arrived in Glasgow and walked into Rattrays cycle shop a little after noon, carrying my embarrassingly de-spoked wheel.

"What happened?" the man behind the counter asked in disbelief. "Get your chain caught in the wheel?"

"Something like that," I muttered. Hot pokers wouldn't get a direct answer to that question out of me. The repairman examined the wheel, then suggested I simply purchase another rim and discard the first, which I did, having them put my old tube and tire onto the new wheel they provided. I was keeping the man who waited on me from going to lunch, and he consequently worked in a blue rage, unable to locate any of the needed tools and parts, swearing as he plowed his way through the parts department. Even done this way, though, the job didn't take too long. Of course, standing in Scotland's largest bike shop, it still did not occur to me to arm myself with spare parts or tools against future problems—surely everything would hold together from now on!

Leaving Rattrays, it seemed strange walking through Glasgow's frowning streets after being in Oban that same morning. It had taken me three days to cover the same distance on Braw Handsel the first time. I was glad when I was on the train again, hurtling back through another clear afternoon toward Oban and the rest of Braw Handsel waiting in the bike shop there.

The sun set just as the train swung into Oban, and by the time I was walking back to my B&B the bay seemed filled with ink, while the mountains of Mull lay stark and crystal clear under the floating moon. I felt a great energy boiling up in me: to get Braw Handsel functioning again, to carry me through as much of this wonderous land as possible while such clarity prevailed. Until now, I hadn't realized just how much of this country had been hidden by the constant mist.

There was also a sense of limited time floating about my mind. The Scots I talked with all assured me that the rest of my trip must surely be made in rain and storm, as Scotland was never as dry as it had been during my days there. In fact, though, my trip coincided almost perfectly with Scotland's longest drought in nearly 200 years, perhaps the best piece of luck during the entire trip. I was to get wet, but not for days on end, and for that I was very thankful.

Seven
Of Mountains and Islands
And Old Standing Stones

The next morning I returned to the Oban cycle shop, and in a few minutes had Braw Handsel operating once again. Would everything work, I wondered? Was this new wheel going to last? What else might go wrong? Such thoughts were completely new to me, and the first care-free 500 miles of my trip now seemed like an idyllic but vanished past.

Braw Handsel seemed docile enough, though, as I pushed up the steep hill leading out of Oban and pedaled slowly north. It was very evident that I was coming to the heart of the Scottish Highlands. All around enormous mountains lifted themselves up out of the sea. An excellent example was Beinn Bheithir, a hulking snow-topped peak directly behind the Ballachulish Ferry.

In fact, Beinn Bheithir stands only 3284 feet high, truly a miniscule altitude, yet it still was very impressive. The human eye is an ultimate trickster and, as a result, Scotland offers the visitor magnificent mountain grandeur on a miniature but undetectable scale. All of which is very nice for the cyclist, because you don't have to go so far to enjoy great changes in scenery as you would have to in a country of larger scale.

I enjoyed the view, then rode the ferry across the mouth of Loch Leven for free.

"It's my birthday, lad," explained the boatman.

Then came a brief pedal up the loch for a look at the Pap of Glencoe (2430 feet) and Bidean nam Bian (3766 feet), after which I pedaled on to Fort William through an extremely strong headwind, blithely unaware that I had just set eyes on perhaps the most infamous spot in all Scottish history. I only learned of what I had missed several weeks and many hundreds of miles later, when I picked up John Prebble's fine book, *Glencoe*.

The map of Scotland is covered with the names of glens, i.e. the areas surrounding the rivers and streams that run everywhere throughout this land. The glen of the River Coe is one of the most rugged of these, its east-west course bounded to both north and south by some of Scotland's steepest peaks. Since the time of Robert Bruce, in the early 14th century, the people who lived under the protection of those peaks were equally abrupt members of Clan Donald, the MacDonalds of Glencoe. On Feb. 13, 1692, a party of 128 royal troops, who were lodging with the MacDonalds, under orders turned on their hosts, slaughtering men, women and children alike as a symbol of an inexcusable and bloody sacrifice on the altar of "Mi-run mor ann Gall, the Lowlander's great hatred."

Glencoe is the first of a trilogy of works that painstakingly and brilliantly outline the long process that over the course of 200 years saw the destruction of the Highland clans and the virtual depopulation of the country they inhabited. Officially, the slaughter of Glencoe was sanctioned by the government of William and Mary, who replaced James VII (II of England) on the combined Scottish and English thrones. The clan leader, MacIain, a proud and obstinate man, failed to submit to an oath of allegiance to King William before a prescribed date. MacIain *had* submitted, but this fact was suppressed by the man who pushed for the issuance of "Letters of Fire and Sword" against the clan. The massacre was actually a small battle in an extended conflict for control of Scotland. Prebble explains:

> "The Highland people were once the majority of Scotland's population, a military society that had largely helped to establish and maintain her monarchy. This society, tribal and feudal, could not change itself to meet a changing world, nor did it wish to . . . By 1690 the Highlanders were already regarded by many Lowlanders as an obstacle to the complete political union of England and Scotland, and their obstinate independence of spirit—expressed in their customs, their clothes and their language—had to be broken and humbled. The MacDonalds of Glencoe were early victims of what the Highlanders called *Mi-run mor nan Gall*, the Lowlander's great hatred. Lowland leaders naturally despised what they wished to destroy, and therefore that destruction seemed to be a virtuous necessity . . . The same contempt for the Highlander was responsible for the brutalities that followed Culloden in 1746, and the same indifference to his way of life was shown when the Clearances began 50 years later."

The facts of Glencoe were still unknown to me, as I battled my way up Loch Linnhe toward Fort William, against a headwind that often saw me walking the cycle along the perfectly flat road instead of riding it. After a snack in a little tea shop in Fort William, I turned off the main road to go up Glen Nevis, to the youth hostel located there, at the base of Britain's highest mountain, Ben Nevis.

The Glen Nevis hostel was a larger one than my first one in Tobermory, and was quite filled with people as well. Several of these were cyclists, one little man coming in after whipping off 90 miles.

I thought, "Well, after all, he doesn't have any luggage to speak of, legs like oak trees, probably does this all the time." I had been happy with 46 miles, until this came up. Another cyclist, an American with a high dune-buggy flag mounted on the rear of his bike casually described the repair equipment he was carrying along "just in case." He could easily have built a new bike out of old coat-hangers. I didn't tell him about my repair kit, made up of my faithful wrench and one patch kit.

There was one other guest at the hostel, a rider of a huge motor cycle, who struck me as both strange and sad. He came up for no reason and stated, "Can't place my accent, can you!" Since he sounded like an American trying to talk with his tongue curled up, I had to admit that I couldn't. "Ha," he said, very pleased. "Everyone thinks I'm European." He went on to talk about how much he hated the States, landing heavily on television and pre-processed foods, and applauding his own attempts to disguise his origins. He acted like a man swinging heavily at shadows, and falling down half the time as a result. It seems such a hopeless undertaking to try to cut yourself off from what has shaped you.

The next morning I was up early, and by 8 o'clock was walking the trail that led to the summit of Ben Nevis, Britain's highest peak at 4406 feet. The walk is said to take four hours up, three down. I was pleased to do it in three hours and two. I was less pleased to find the 100-mile view from the summit reduced to a few yards by swirling mist, grieved that if Braw Handsel had not struck on Mull, I would have been here one day earlier, when things were clear as crystal. It was very cold on top, and the several feet of snow there made walking quite difficult—especially as I was doing it in glass-smooth track shoes.

Hiking, or any other outdoor activity, is different in Great Britain than in the States, because Britain is such a small island, in the middle of cold seas. As a result, the weather can change, and change sharply, in an incredibly short time. At the start of my walk up the trail the summit of Ben Nevis was clear. Yet two-thirds of the way up, a biting cold mist came down all around me. Suddenly I wished very much that I had thought to follow the advice on one of the hostel signs, which spoke about carrying a parka. Then, almost at the top, the snow covered the trail, which I immediately lost.

Once on the broad, domed summit, I spotted a yellow rescue hut, and began walking straight for it, the mist eddying all about. Luckily it eddied away from my path at the right moment, since I was blithely about to walk right over a verticle edge.

I was back at the youth hostel by early afternoon, glad to be down in the warm valley again. I was less pleased to realize that the hostel was shut. (They close each afternoon so the warden can leave.) Luckily, the warden returned for something, and I was able to retrieve my pink slip and put in some miles—45 to be exact—to the next hostel at Garramore.

The day's travel was essentially along a long, straight line, stretching from Ben Nevis west along Loch Eil past the head of Loch Shiel, then along Loch Eilt and several stretches of ocean before reaching the hostel. There were things to see along the way—the giant pulp mill polluting the air below Ben Nevis, the monument to Bonny Prince Charley at Loch Shiel, the beautiful ocean coast and a view of that island with the most lovely of names: Muck.

The most interesting site of the day was the monument to Bonny Prince Charley. A tall column with a statue of the prince stands at the head of narrow Loch Shiel, marking the spot where the Young Pretender first flew his standard on Aug. 19, 1745, and called on the Highlanders to help him regain the combined thrones of England and Scotland for his family, the Stuarts.

Prince Charles Stewart was the son of James VII of Scotland/James II of England, "The Old Pretender," who was driven into exile on Dec. 23, 1688, because of his leanings toward Catholicism. The Old Pretender returned to Scotland in 1715, to lead the Jacobite rebellion against Charles I and reclaimed the throne for himself and the Stuart line, but little came of it. His son Charles, however, fared far better against Charles II of England, actually fighting his way to within 80 miles of London before the drive of his Jacobite cause and followers weakened and failed. On the retreat, he still managed to rebuild his army once again, only to guide it to nearly complete destruction at Culloden Fields, near Inverness on April 16, 1746.

The Prince then melted away to five months of elusive hiding from the English in the Western Highlands and islands before returning to France, leaving his highland followers to face the government's enthusiastic destruction of their culture, society and very lives. Even the kilt and pipes were banned by punishment of death. Again, the visitor can only wonder in disbelief at such events arising out of such quiet, lovely surroundings.

The Garramore hostel was much smaller than that at Glen Nevis, with a nice little store and a men's bunk room that was entirely empty. In a way, it was nice that the hostel at Glen Nevis had been so crowded. It made me more appreciative of the virtually empty one here. I promptly brought Braw Handsel inside, spread all my things out over three bunks, and made myself right at home. My self-made dinner of rice and curry, with a can of pudding for dessert, seemed like a feast. Then came a nice hot shower, and the pleasure of reading in my private dorm long past the lights-out rule. Perhaps the sybaritic nature of this, my third hostel, was offered to me by the gods to make up for the surprise that greeted me the next morning. Outside, it was raining. I mean, water was coming out of the sky overhead —quite a grey sky I might add—making everything underneath those clouds wet, including me.

This will never do, I thought, water dripping from my nose. In *my* Scotland it *never* rains, or at least it hadn't up until now. So how dare it start to do so? At this rate, I might even have to use one of the three sets of raingear I was carrying. How awful!

I pedaled the short distance to Mallaig, enjoying—despite the rain—the sandy beaches and aquamarine water that I passed, then took the ferry to Armadale, on the Isle of Skye.

Skye is an island of light: light playing through the clouds, on the hills, off the water. It is almost as if the sweeping vistas of the island, and the island's rather drab, basic brown, were created more as background than as subject matter for the light that shifts and redefines itself everywhere.

As I pedaled the 17 miles from the ferry to Broadford and a youth hostel there, I found myself either disappointed with or unattuned to Skye's physical reality—I thought Mull was more striking. But I was fascinated by the light, which complimented the island's spare features. The rain stopped, leaving lovely storm-clouds about, which sent a patch-work quilt of shadow and sunlight slipping silently over the island. I also was caught up at last by spring, evident here in the roadside's green border and the grass sprouting through burned-black heather, resembling emerald shards on velvet.

I was very stiff from the exertions of the day before, and was quite glad when Broadford came into view, stretched out in a random line along Broadford Bay, with the great red granite mound of Ben-na-Cailleach behind. Deciding to have a good dinner for a change, I stopped at a butcher shop for a slab of "frying steak," then dashed for the youth hostel as a black cloud swept over the town, pouring heavy rain in its path.

The hostel pointed toward Loch Carron. A glance in that direction, toward mainland Scotland, offered still another fine vista of peaks and showering clouds penetrated by shafts of brilliant sunlight here and there. The afternoon and evening continued to alternate rain with sun, offering the hostel guests ample entertainment just outside the window.

I stayed on Skye for three more nights, spending one at Dunvegan and two more at Uig, waiting for the ferry to the islands of the outer Hebrides, Lewis and Harris. For some reason, or rather for no real reason, I did not enjoy Skye as much as I expected to. Probably it was simply due to a passing dull mood—I felt a great deal of lassitude while on Skye—or perhaps to the fact that Skye is touted as *the* must-see island of Scotland.

I thought Mull the more interesting of the two, the scenery more immediate and the inhabited portions far less developed for the presence of tourists. Skye offered perfectly nice surroundings, but I never felt really in touch with the place. For example, I was passing two flat-topped peaks called Macleod's Tables, and I vaguely recalled the story connected with them. A man of power, either Lowlander or English, put on a sumptuous meal in a great hall with magnificent settings, then turned to Macleod of Dunvegan and said, "You'll not have seen the likes of this in your far-off home."

"But we have, and better," replied Macleod. "Come and see if I don't speak the truth."

The man came, and Macleod took him from Dunvegan to a feast spread on tables atop the great flat-topped mountain nearby, the men of his clan serving as living candelabra in a circle about the peak, the stars overhead a magnificent roof. The visiting nobleman was forced to agree with Macleod's statement.

At the Uig hostel I enjoyed playing Scrabble with one of two New Zealand girls who were there. Time and time again, I ran across girls from New Zealand and Australia, traveling in pairs, venturing from their homes on tours around the world that were to last as long as five years. Usually they secure some means of transport to Europe, then work their way on around the world by whatever means they can, returning home far older and vastly more experienced and aware of the world they live in.

This seems to me to be a form of travel largely unique to girls from these two countries. They undertake these five-year plans because of the difficulty they face earning enough money in their home economies to see them through a shorter but more expensive, non-working trip to Europe. American girls certainly don't seem to go in for this prolonged journeying abroad for the most part.

Whenever I met girls from other countries doing this I found myself fascinated. They always struck me as amazingly brave to throw themselves into such a venture, often without any sort of economic life-line to pull them back to home, confident that they will make out quite nicely, thank you, in all of the myriad situations they encounter.

Finally, during a lazy day's ride around the tip of Skye and back to Uig, I encountered my first peat diggers. The B&B at which I had stayed in Dunvegan had offered an evening fire fueled by lumps of peat—brick-sized blocks of light, fibrous material that burned with a distinctive, meadowy smell. Now, pedaling along a narrow road across the end of the island from Uig, I passed two old couples hard at work digging the fuel up out of the ground. I stopped and leaned Braw Handsel up against a stone bridge, then walked back and asked if I might take a photo. They said sure, not even breaking the rhythm of their work while talking to me.

Peat as a term refers to what is produced when plant material accumulates under anaerobic conditions with poor aeration. As a result it builds up instead of decomposing. The Highlands and Hebrides islands of Scotland offer just the right conditions for peat to accumulate. Over one million acres of Scotland are buried, in many places to an average depth of seven feet, under blanket-bogs of peat.

The formation of peat depends in large part on its staying very wet;

People who depend on peat for fuel must dig tons to see themselves through a year.

consequently digging peat is a very sloppy, messy affair. The two couples were working as a rhythmic team, the men slicing and lifting the blocks of peat out of the ground, the women stacking them for drying. Each little town and village in a peat area will have its own recognized area for digging peat, and woe betide anyone who ventures into the peatlands of another town.

The peat blocks resemble bricks of mud more than anything else, but once they are dry their vegetable origin comes clear again. A block of peat supplies about two-thirds the heat that a similar weight of coal would yield, so the people who depend on it for heat must dig tons to see themselves through a year.

In large part, my lack of enthusiasm for Skye may have come from an intense desire to reach Lewis. There I expected to see the Standing Stones of Callanish, Scotland's answer to Stonehenge. Once I was on a ferry for the Outer Hebrides, I found my energy and interest increasing with each mile of foaming wake we stretched out behind us. After 38 of these, I found myself across the Little Minch, disembarking at Tarbert, on the Isle of Harris.

Each of the Scottish islands appeared more barren than the previous, but surely nothing could be a rockier waste than the Isle of Harris. Coming into Tarbert's little harbor, it seemed we were edging out way into a rockpile that provided a shelf for the little town, then leaped upward to form Harris's tumbled, mountainous backbone. The lines of small shops and little cottages sitting by the water, with the bright yellow of a plant called gorse lending it color, seemed warm and friendly, but all the rest of the island that was visible seemed to declare that the town was a horrendous mistake in location.

The Isles of Lewis and Harris are seen to be political creations after the briefest of glances at a map of the Outer Hebrides. They are all part of the same island, southern Harris lying in Inverness-shire, northern Lewis in Ross-shire. That they are all one island is a fact, yet to a traveler, particularly a cyclist, they are as different as night and day. Harris is all verticals falling off into the sea, while Lewis is as flat as a brown rug spread on a floor. Where Harris at least has rocks to give shelter from the wind, Lewis offers nothing of the sort. Not a tree or a bush stands up there, it seems, and the wind is a constant element, a fact of reality like gravity or magnetism. The people are even said by some to differ between the two. The people of Lewis have Viking blood in their past, and are tall and fair, while Harrismen tend to be shorter and darker, showing their Celtic background.

One couple on the ferry even mentioned their belief that men from one portion of the island became gentler and more friendly under the influence of alcohol, while those from the other became mean and surly, prone to fight. Unfortunately, I failed to carefully note which group of reactions went with which portion of the island, so I was forced to refrain from drinking copious amounts of alcohol with citizens from either place.

Tarbert was an attractive little place, with its several shops for tartans and woolens—these islands are famous for such products. Wanting to get to Stornoway, 38 miles away in Lewis, however, I left almost immediately, pedaling and pushing Braw Handsel up over the hills of Harris in a day so warm I was down to my single shirt and still hot.

As I went on one long uphill grade, pushing the bike, there was an old man carrying tools for cutting peat. He was the one who told me about towns having their own peating areas, and his was far up in the hills. I felt somewhat embarrassed, my work to get the cycle over the hills so frivolous compared to this man's far greater effort to get just his own aged body up them. My shiny cycle and bright saddle bags and other slick equipment all seemed to shout, "Callow youth here," in contrast to this essential old fellow. But he smiled over at me, almost as if he felt my thoughts.

"It's good to travel when you're young," he said. "I did some myself. Went clear to Glasgow. That was a few years back, though."

Perhaps it was, but I was pleased that he also had his chance to travel, and cared to mention it to me. I made some comment about how rocky Harris was.

The old man smiled, nodded agreement, then said, "They say God built the earth here, and here he left the shavings and splinters." What a nice explanation.

Finally the climb from Tarbert came to an end, and there followed a long, long downhill run, the road snaking by peating grounds dug in the past or being worked currently by men and women alone or in groups. At last I found myself on the barely undulating flatness of Lewis, the hills of Harris a line of rock behind me. It was almost as though I had crossed the dotted line that as youngsters we all knew separated countries of the world, so abrupt was the change. I pedaled on along Loch Seaforth, then over a narrow stretch of land and along Loch Erisort. The warmth of the morning was giving way to a dull, colder afternoon, and I was making the acquaintance with the winds of Lewis, ubiquitous winds that are probably the culprits that blew Lewis so flat.

For some reason I was painting a far fairer picture in my mind of my destination, the town of Stornoway, largest town in Ross-shire. Perhaps because of the flat drabness of my surroundings, I saw Stornoway as a

The brochs of Scotland's North and islands seem to have been places of defense, all following a similar plan.

green town, with tree-lined streets, good restaurants, a friendly B&B just waiting for me and a laundromat waiting for my clothing on every corner. I had not seen a laundromat since Glasgow, two weeks before, and my limited wardrobe definitely needed the attentions of a good washing machine.

As a result of all this mental dreaming, Stornoway, in reality a nice enough little port of some 5000 inhabitants, seemed quite disappointing upon arrival. Finding a B&B was difficult. The one I did find housed a couple who seemed distinctly uninterested in offering me the cheer and comfort I hoped for. Needless to say, there were no laundromats "just around the corner" or anywhere else in Stornoway.

As usual, a bath, meal and sleep served to revise my view of the world. The next morning Stornoway looked just fine as I rode through it, on my way to my next goal—the Standing Stones of Callanish. Evidently the gods decided to favor anyone heading for Callanish this particular day. They served up a beautiful tail wind that blew me over hill and dale clear to my destination, 15 miles away. (Of course, the aforesaid gods immediately reconsidered such generosity, and throughout the following day sent a wind whistling into my face no matter which way I was heading.)

Standing Stones: They seem cryptic messages from a past before history, addressed not to men of the future but to the gods and shadowy

69

presences these early philosophers recognized in their environment. As a result, the message is obscure—perhaps unfathomable—for today's visitor, but the strength of conviction and power behind that message is quite undiluted. The statement's meaning is indecipherable, but its force is like a beacon of faith radiating its light to the farthest reaches of space.

I came over a hill, spotted the strung-out town of Callanish across the small valley ahead, then noticed a small circle of stones on the crest of a little hill to my left. They seemed like creatures out of myth, met for some fell conference only to be frozen in place by some implacable power for the rest of eternity. I glanced once again toward the town of Callanish, and realized that there, on the crest behind that small village, stood the truly huge stone circle of Callanish, forceful even at this distance.

The Standing Stones of Callanish were raised sometime during the late Stone Age and Early Bronze Age, between 3000 B.C. and 1500 B.C. Archeologists believe the circle represents a long period of development, and that it was used for cult practices long into the Bronze Age.

In plain description, Callanish consists of a circle of stones 37 feet in diameter, circling a megalithic-chambered cairn or tomb, 21 feet in diameter, surrounded by a kerb of stone. A central stone rises from this kerb to a height of more than 15 feet, aligned with two avenues of stones that north-south, while two additional lines of stones radiate to the east and west. Some 47 stones still stand at Callanish. Scientists are certain that there were more here at one time, but they have vanished.

Such a bare description, however, in no way conveys the mood of Callanish. The visitor finds himself riding through a town of thatched huts and small cottages, and cannot help but feel how primitive—how *quaint*— a place this is, far removed from the realities of the modern world. But then you reach the stones, sitting at the top of the hill at the end of the road, and suddenly it is forcibly realized that the town behind is as modern as yesterday's newspaper in comparison with these silent rocks.

The wind was whipping over the hill as I walked in amongst the stones. The sky overhead was a plowed field of blue-black clouds, a perfect counter-point for the rude, silent stones below. Where Stonehenge is unbelievably massive, its components great square blocks that could only have been handled by giants, Callanish's stones are far lighter, with a great deal more character.

It was, of course, sheer romanticism on my part, but I felt a great power about these stones and their mute design, an unwavering attention to a view of the universe completely forgotten by the last hundred generations of human development. They are so mute, so silent, so unperturbed by the passage of time and the wash of nature's forces, that I for one could not help but wonder if the men who created this site might not have known something of importance about the world that we have forgotten, have lost.

I spent an hour at Callanish, then hurried several miles up the road, working against a stiff head wind now, in order to see another feature of the area, an ancient *broch* near the town of Carloway, seven miles away.

Dating from the beginning of the Christian era, the brochs of Scotland's North and islands seem to have been places of defense for family-sized units of a dominant aristocracy, similar to the feudal castles of a later age. They all follow a similar plan, consisting of an inner area 20 to 35 feet across, protected by a circular double wall with a stairway inside and rising to a height of 30 or 40 feet with a single easily defended doorway allowing access. Amazingly, the whole structure, which looks like a giant beehive without a top, built of worked or unworked stone, does not have a drop of mortar in it.

The next day the 17 short miles back to Stornoway from Callanish seemed by far the longest miles of the trip, courtesy of the stiff, unending headwind that pinned me to the road, making the flat roadway seem like a path up a vertical wall. Finally it was done, however, and where before I was disappointed with Stornoway, now the little port looked pretty good.

The following morning, I boarded the ferry for Ullapool, three hours away across the North Minch. The wind was extremely stiff as we emerged from Stornoway's protected harbor, and several people promptly were ill in the stuffy, crowded passenger area. Of course, I wasn't ill at all, being such a superb traveler and seaman. I wasn't, that is, until the large ship began rolling from side to side, pitching in a corkscrew motion as well. So much for at least one intrepid traveler's intrepid stomach and breakfast.

Eight
Ullapool to Ullapool

I'm sure that seasickness has transformed the destinations of many travelers into something akin to Nirvana, or the Pearly Gates. As Ullapool was a very attractive spot in its own right, my arrival there seemed doubly blessed. It lies on a point of land jutting out into the mouth of Loch Broom, creating a fine harbor in front of the town. The slopes immediately behind the white houses of the town were green with grass, while farther back came the brown of heather and beyond stood grey-to-black, snow-topped peaks, all lying this day under heavy black clouds scudding by overhead, backlit by the sun.

There is a youth hostel there, right on the harbor, and you can sit in its community kitchen and dining room, looking out the window at the whitecaps bouncing around on Loch Broom. A number of boats were anchored just in front of the hostel, one almost entirely underwater, swamped by the blowing waves.

I was glad the hostel was as close to the ferry wharf as it was. I was still not feeling quite right, due in part to the silly ways of people with cars. As soon as the ferry came close to shore, everyone ran down to the car deck and gunned their vehicles to life. As a result, the ferry belched out a great cloud of exhaust fumes when the gangplank was finally let down, and everyone came out choking and half suffocated, including the lone cyclist stuck among the cars.

As I was in some doubt as to which direction the trip should proceed, I spoke with the woman who ran the hostel. She suggested that I make a loop back inland to Kyle of Lochalsh, with its ferry to Skye, and then back to Ullapool along the coast. The country was beautiful, she said, and I really shouldn't miss it.

The next day I left some weighty equipment with this helpful woman, and managed to reel off 61 miles in as easy and delightful a day of travel as any I was to experience in Scotland. It is unlikely that there could actually be almost 60 miles of downhill slant, from the top of the hill at the head of Loch Broom to an independent hostel at Achnashellach, but it certainly felt like there were. Perhaps I was blessed with a constant tail wind.

The weather was beautiful throughout this day. I rode through the upper end of Loch Broom, a very green place smothered with trees, that seemed like a piece of Switzerland set down in these western Highlands.

There came a steep climb, and then I was at my first stop, the Falls of Measach and Corrieshalloch Gorge. The Falls drop 150 feet from one level of the gorge to another, between fern-covered vertical walls of schist. With the sun coming and going behind passing white clouds, the light in the narrow gorge was constantly changing, and with it the color of the water and lush vegetation. It all combined to create a very lovely visual symphony.

Also lovely was the blonde girl standing on the suspension bridge from which you can see the falls to best advantage. Finding her blonde and beautiful despite the sweatshirt and jeans she was wearing, I managed to dredge up some remark about the canyon, instead of one about how madly I was in love with her. But I wouldn't want to offend anyone-particularly anyone like her husky husband who was standing at the other end of the bridge. Evidently no one was offended, because we all began to talk together.

How often does it happen that you meet people with whom you very simply "click"? We ended talking together for almost two hours, and I found these two as fascinating and attractive a couple as I've ever met.

Not only was the woman beautiful, but her name was Heather, a particularly deadly combination for any properly appreciative male, I'm sure. Heather and her husband, Allan, were Australians, from a little town in New South Wales. They, like so many others from their part of the world, were on a five-year plan of travel around the world. So far they had spent two years in America. (Heather would do office work, while Allan earned money as a baker, a line of work that allows him to find a job almost anywhere he cares to look.) Now they were living in London.

Allan and Heather were covering England and Scotland in an absolutely super BMC travel van, made over from an electrician's van, boasting such amenities as a small stove and cooking cabinet, a well-stocked little refrigerator and color-coordinated purple floor-rug and hand towels. After Britain they intended to move to the continent, to travel and work there. Then they would push their way back home, seeing as much of the world as they could along the way.

We talked about all sorts of things, over the tea and crackers they invited me to join them for: about doing stone rubbings in and around London, the travels they planned through Europe and Africa, the cost of cars in New Zealand, the places they had most enjoyed in Scotland so far, and so on and so forth. I don't really think that these topics were the source of the warm friendliness we seemed to feel between us, however. Rather, I think that our "click" came from the enthusiasm we all felt for such pursuits, and the unspoken support such enthusiastic talk gave all of us for our various ongoing enterprises. (It always amazes me how much energy can come from supportive people. I can only be grateful that so much flow arose from a chance encounter between strangers on a suspension bridge over a narrow, green gorge. Perhaps this, as much as the obliging tail wind, sped me on my way after we finally parted company.)

From the Measach Falls I pedaled southeast past the Glascarnach reservoir to the little town of Garve, then turned southwest to ride down Strath Bran. This part of the day belonged to the clouds overhead, great white puffs with constantly shifting turrets and battlements. The gently rolling mountains on each side of my route served as great heather-covered screens for the play of light and dark under the passing clouds, much the same as had happened the week before on Skye.

The country became increasingly beautiful as the day wore on, a wonderful blend of warmth, stands of green pines, a babbling stream at my side and farther off the clouds playing with the mountains. Many of these peaks marking the skyline of the broad valley were definitely noteworthy. Yet the map marked them as not even as high as Mount Tamalpias on the San Francisco Bay. Much of Strath Bran and Strath Carron struck me as similar to country I had seen years before in Wyoming, yet the vistas were less than a sixth in size. I lost all sense of time and enjoyed the country as I passed by.

My body, however, wanted to arrive somewhere—mainly off the cycle for the day—so I asked about lodging at the Achnasheen Hotel. They had nothing that I could afford, but the hostess there, after serving me tea and some sandwiches, suggested that I try a private hostel "just 11 miles down the road." I guess she didn't realize that I was traveling by bike. However, it proved an easy 11 miles. The road still provided a downhill tail wind, and I enjoyed the final minutes of light to the fullest. Fluffy clouds capped the peaks of the long valley, and the setting sun turned the heather covering the ranges of Glen Carron on my left to a gold-red, with blinding-white snow patches on the ridge crests.

The Achnashellach hostel, a private one, was quite different from the other hostels I frequented in Scotland. It was run along far more informal lines, wasn't as spick and span as the proper SYHA hostels, but as a result seemed more human and interesting. There were books and magazines scattered everywhere, and several men and women were living there on a permanent basis.

The next morning I pedaled off into another beautiful day, heading down Glen Carron, past a mirror-smooth Loch Dughaill, enjoying the warm sunlight and bursting energy of this bright spring day. A cloud canopy followed me down the valley, suggesting poor weather under its expanse, but it never caught up to ruin the morning. After a pleasant ride down the gentle slope of Glen Carron I came to the head of Loch Carron, which connects with the sea.

I glanced out over the water, and was startled to see what seemed the curving back of some sea creature knifing through the water. It disappeared, then reappeared, arching its way through the water, and proceeded in this manner in grand majesty up the loch. It must have been a porpoise making an inspection of this inland arm of the sea. If this had occured in Loch Ness, I would have instantly identified the shape as that of the Monster.

A little further along, the road rose up from the loch once again, while an old, planted forest ran up and down the hillside on both sides of the road. As I pushed the bike up this grade, I could see long vistas down the aisles of space between the trees, and in one of them I spotted a deer, down the hill to my right, exactly the same color as the trunks of the spruce trees that hid its wanderings. It grew aware of being watched, and finally bolted off through the trees. It bolted, but I could follow its progress for a long distance, as its flight intersected the open aisles.

Two low passes later I came to the most beautiful, most impressive view of the entire trip. I ground the bike to a halt, and simply stood and stared trying to take it all in.

On my left ran Loch Duich, perfectly described in the *Blue Guide* as "savagely grand." Beyond it, there rose a jagged range of peaks known as the Five Sisters of Kintail, leaping—if you will allow me to be carried away with typical Scottish enthusiasm—to a height of 3500 feet. Just beyond the foot of my hill stood Eilean Donan Castle, on a little peninsula jutting out into the loch. To my right stretched Loch Alsh, with the mountains of Skye beyond, far more impressive from my present vantage point than they had seemed on the island itself. The warmth of the day, the slant of the sun coloring the far ridges a rich blue-black, the ocean below a deep shade of blue-green, the fresh grass on the nearer hills bright green, set off by the stunning yellow of acres of gorse plants: it was all quite perfect, a vista of absolutely stunning impact. It seemed as though Scotland had decided to show this touring cyclist just exactly what it could produce in the way of natural scenery when it chose to.

I stood and absorbed the scene laid out before me as best I could for almost twenty minutes. Then a noise caught my attention. Looking back up the road, I saw a slow, heavy truck loaded with a great mound of logs creeping over the crest of the hill and starting down toward me. Noting how very slow it was, I decided that I would like to keep ahead of it, particularly on the quite steep, narrow length of road running down the hill toward Loch Alsh. I went plunging off down the hill, and only then noticed the backhoe that was working on a ditch in a curve of the road. It was just starting to swing its rear out into the roadway, and I realized that I would have to stop or run into it.

Convulsively, I squeezed Braw Handsel's handbrakes as hard as I could, fighting all the downward momentum of the cycle, its heavy luggage and me. Then occured the damndest freak accident of the trip. The rear caliper brakes, which are supposed to grip the metal rim of the wheel, came under such pressure and torque that they slipped off the rim and dug into the rubber of the wheel, neatly flipped the tire up out of the rim, scooted underneath and blew up the inner tube.

I was just about motionless by then, aware that something was very wrong from the sounds going on below me, looking up at that backhoe operator who was looking at me. When the tube blew, I could see my fright mirrored in his face: The thing went off like a bomb, and scared the hell out of both of us. In the silence that followed, I thought I heard Braw Handsel chuckling maliciously, but I could have been mistaken.

So there I stood, highly embarrassed, astride a cycle with a rear tire as flat as flat can be, and the backhoe operator staring at me in dumb amazement. Manfully, I got off Braw Handsel and wheeled my injured cycle down the hill, while the rear wheel made complaining, squelching noises. The whole way down I wondered just how I was going to deal with this new development. I had never changed a bike tire before.

At the bottom of the hill I found a shady spot, then went about the business of changing Braw Handsel's tire. I turned the cycle over to get at the rear wheel, took it off, then got out the two tire irons Mr. MacDonald had given me in Edinburgh. The idea is to deftly pry an edge of the tire with one of these, slip the other in and run it all the way around the rim, disengaging the tire and slipping the whole thing off the rim. It is easier in theory than in practice, I found. The tube was utterly ruined.

After slipping on a new tube—thank goodness I picked a spare up in Stromness—I was set. Or I would have been set if the freak accident had not involved the brake locking the wheel, so that it skidded several yards on one spot. There was no tire left on the skidded spot and the thin inner tube came in direct contact with the ground through the resulting hole. I very much wanted to go to see Eilean Donan Castle, three miles to my left, but I didn't feel I could trust the cycle to get me there and clear back to Kyle of Lochalsh. I needed to get there to catch a ferry across to Skye and the town of Kyleakin, where I had heard there was a cycle shop.

While pondering my sad state, an energetic woman came running out from one of the nearby whitewashed houses to chase a hungry cow out of her prize vegetable patch. After she managed this, she came back to talk with me, inspecting my repair job and offering me tea. I didn't want to impose—there was no real reason for this nice lady to serve tea to such a stranger. However, I did ask if I might leave Braw Handsel with her while I walked down to the castle. She said certainly. It was a pleasant three-mile walk to Eilean Donan, although as I went I realized just how hot the day was, down here at sea level, without a breath of air stirring.

Eilean Donan Castle, one of the most famous of all Scottish castles, is a 20th century reconstruction of an 800-year-old structure that was battered almost to bits by an English warship in 1719, during an abortive Jacobite uprising. Today it is fully restored to its former state, affording the visitor an exciting leap back into the past, when castle walls had to be thick and strong against the foes outside. I think the castle's fame comes as much from its setting in Loch Duich as from its impressive walls and battlements, however.

I enjoyed the castle, then stopped in the little town of Dornie for a roll of tape with which I planned to patch Braw Handsel. A man then offered me a lift in his car, and as it really was very hot, I gladly accepted. As we rode along, he spoke of how awful the weather was: "Too dry." All around me the hills were far greener than they ever are in my native California, but he went on about how terribly brown they seemed to him. I was sorry for his hills, but I could only hope they would have plenty of chance to get browner, at least until I'd finished cycling through his country.

The tape on the rear wheel gave me greater confidence of making it to Kyle of Lochalsh, and in fact I did with no further problems, except one minor one. Pedaling along, I noticed that the inside of my left knee was quite sore. It seemed to hurt with each push on the pedal, and was distinctly uncomfortable. I put it out of my mind, however, as I rode down toward the pretty little town of Kyle of Lochalsh, that lies on one side of the narrow straits of Kyle Akin. I was forced to wonder what sort of cycle shop was in Kyleakin across the narrow channel on Skye, and if possibly it could supply me with a new tire. After all, the cycle shop in Oban, a much larger town, proved practically useless the last time I had to fix Braw Handsel.

I took the ferry across the narrow straits, and after a bit of searching discovered the small bike shop of Mr. McDougal. He proved to be a very nice young man, who seemed even nicer when he rummaged about a bit inside his tiny shed of a shop and came up with just the proper tire for my cycle. We slipped it on, and I thanked him profusely, then wandered back into Kyleakin, looking for supper and a place to stay.

My decision to stay in a B&B, instead of at the youth hostel back in Kyle Lochalsh, was based on finding a hot bath to soak my knee. I managed to locate an inexpensive B&B run by a very pleasant, cooperative woman, which offered this weary traveler a nice, long tub to soak in.

As I lay in the hot water, I couldn't help but think how lucky I was to have experienced this second, weird breakdown, so near a source of repair. What would have happened if anything like this were to happen in the deserted regions to the north, near Cape Wrath? (Of course I didn't know it at the time, but I was destined to find out.)

The next morning I was on the slanting cement ferry landing, waiting to cross back to the mainland, when I noticed just how loose the rear brake was. Deciding to take care of such a problem early for a change, I went back to Mr. McDougal a second time, and the problem was corrected. I again thanked him, and bade him what I thought was a final good-bye. (As you shall see, I was mistaken in this belief.)

It was a drizzly, rainy day, not very pleasant for traveling. I crossed on the ferry, rode around the point from Loch Alsh to Loch Carron, and was once again pedaling along the shore where I had seen the porpoise or whatever, when Braw Handsel decided to try to give me a break from travel for the rest of the day. Racing down a hill, I came onto a narrow two-inch cut in the pavement running across the road for what purpose I cannot imagine.

"Thunk-thunk" went the bike wheels as I crossed the space, "Wow, that was pretty hard" I thought, and Braw Handsel agreed with the "chunk-pinngg" sound that had grown all too familiar on Mull. Broken spoke No. 9 for the trip. And of course, it was on the same side as the gear block, making it impossible for me to repair the cycle myself, even if I knew how.

I knew that I had to return directly to the cycle shop in Kyleakin. But the question was, how? Kyleakin was several hills and quite a few miles away by now, and it seemed prudent to keep my broken spokes down to one by not riding that far. I decided the only course was to get to the head of Loch Carron, catch the next train whenever it came through, return to Kyleakin, fix the bike, and try again. All of which would take at least a day. It was also starting to rain harder now. Great.

So often, however, bad luck seems to be balanced by good. (Unfortunately, though, the reverse also seems to be true.) That seemed the case in my previous problems with Braw Handsel—each breakdown could have proved far worse, I thought—and the pattern held true now. I was pushing the bike along the loch, water dripping down my neck, when I looked up and saw a train coming around the curve of shore on the line of track that ran between me and the water. Now I would have to wait until tomorrow, I groaned. But wait. The train was slowing down. Why? There was no reason that I could see, but it was stopping at a tiny, deserted station.

"Hey," I hollered to a man leaning out of the last car. "Can I get a ride back to Kyle of Lochalsh?"

"Sure," he answered, "if you can hurry."

And hurry I did, up over a five-foot fence, somehow levering Braw Handsel and all my equipment up over in a single hoist, and hustling it all into the baggage car. The cost of the ride was minimal, and I was back in Kyleakin knocking on Mr. McDougal's door within an hour.

Mr. McDougal was at lunch, and asked me to wait. My mood during that wait became rather darkened by his musing that he doubted he had the proper gizmo to get the gearblock off and fix the broken spoke. Blast, the same problem as at Oban, I thought.

Mr. McDougal finished his lunch at last, searched about in his little shack of a shop, and made my day by finding just the proper gizmo that was needed. My cycle was fixed in 15 minutes, and again we found ourselves saying good-bye, for the third time. We each expressed hope, in a friendly way, that we would not be seeing each other again in the near future.

In order to capitalize on my good fortune, I decided to take the train back to the head of Loch Carron—an excusable lapse in motivation, I thought, considering the circumstances—and attempt to complete the trip I had planned for the day, to a hostel in Glen Torridon. All went well, and despite getting off the train at five o'clock, and the constant drizzle, I felt eager to travel.

As I labored along, the water dripping off me and clouds swirling about overhead, I couldn't help but think that it was weather such as this, rather than the gentle, fair weather I had enjoyed for so much of the trip, that produced Scotland's horrendously bloody history. All about me, great black cliffs frowned down through cold, wet air under a turbulent canopy of dark cloud, offering a spare, lean, violent beauty, the perfect backdrop for a bloody scene from Shakespeare, or the far bloodier scenes of actual history.

I was miles away from the last habitation I had seen on Loch Kishorn, climbing up a long slant and grumping at the roughness of the road, when

The driver of the library bus is a purveyor of news, information and gossip through the back roads of Scotland.

it seemed as though the gods decided on a massive good-humored joke. I came, miraculously, to macadam as smooth as skin and black as night; so new that it might have been unwinding from a spool just over the hill ahead of me, to be wound up behind as soon as I passed. The bike seemed to sail along up the hill on this surface.

All too soon, though, my mystery road came to an end, with no sign of the equipment that had created it, nor any possible reason for that creation. I left it behind with regret, and continued on over rougher pavement into the darkening wet night. It was a relief to reach the Torridon hostel hours later, with its offering of food and warmth. By now my knee was hurting again, and I found myself increasingly cold, hardly surprising as I was dripping wet and it was the middle of the night.

The next two days were spent getting back to Ullapool, and happily, they contained no more rain for me, despite the canopy of grey cloud that roofed the sky.

In the little town of Poolewe, on the shores of Loch Ewe, I stopped to inspect the Ross & Cromarty County library bus. The bus, a large and surprisingly complete library on wheels, makes its rounds to remote villages throughout the brown moorland and bare rock of this county that stretches from coast to coast of Scotland. The driver of a library bus such as this, or of the several meat and produce vans one sees, is the purveyor of all pertinent news, information and gossip through the back roads of Scotland. What a nice innovation.

A short distance later, I stopped at Inverewe Gardens, the creation of a madman with a will of iron named Osgood MacKenzie. He must have been mad to think he could create a tropical garden on the rocky shores of Loch Ewe, a spot on the same 58th parallel as Canada's Hudson Bay and Siberia. And he had a will of iron to make his dream come true. With incredible labor this man began the task, in 1862, of bringing tons of fertile topsoil to his rocky estate, where he planted tropical flowering plants from all over the world. Today, on more than 2000 acres, these plants are thriving in such profusion that you wonder if this can be rugged Scotland, not some tropical island. It was a grim dark day, yet even so the plants at Inverewe seemed bright and gay. How amazing it must be to walk among them on a really bright sunny day!

I spent the night in Aultbea on Loch Ewe, in a quite comfortable B&B. For the first time I arranged to have dinner by phone, but wondered if it would prove worth the cost. (At a price of roughly $5 for dinner, bed and breakfast, I was complaining?) After a meal of hot soup, pancakes, potatoes, beef stew, carrots and two helpings of hot pudding and ice cream, I decided that I hadn't made a bad choice.

The next day I covered 45 miles in six hours of hilly travel, a paltry distance and time for any real biker, but close to my best speed of the trip. I also pushed my distance traveled by cycle in Scotland to cover 1000 miles. This, and the lovely country I passed through, should have been more than enough to make this a happy day, but events conspired against any joy. Throughout the day there was a whipping head wind that seemed to glue the bike to the road, and as the day progressed my knee became more and more inoperable.

The wind was at its worst on a magnificent downhill run beside Little Loch Broom. This downhill went for several miles, an absolutely beautiful stretch for cycling, neither too steep nor too shallow. However, the wind was blowing so hard into my face that it negated the hill. I had to pedal, in first gear, all the way down to move at all.

As for the knee, it simply hurt, whenever I put downward pressure on my left leg. This set off all sorts of worries in my mind about what would happen if it got any worse, distracting me from the countryside about me.

There was one stretch of downhill, however, where all my attention came back to what was going on around me, at least for a little while. The wind wasn't quite so bad, and I was going along at quite a good clip when Braw Handsel began making noises like one of the innumerable lambs that wander free with their mothers all over the Highland countryside. I couldn't believe it. My cycle, sounding like a bleating lamb of all things.

I glanced to the rear, and discovered that I was maligning my good cycle quite unfairly for a change. The sound *was* bleating, coming from a tiny wad of cotton racing after me on four flying legs, just under the rear of the bike, trying like all get out to keep up with me.

Evidently, little lambs not being too smart, they tend to track on the biggest thing around them, that usually being mother. This little one, glancing up from feeding when I went tearing by, tracked on me instead, and with unthinking obedience had instantly raced after "mother," no doubt wondering what all the rush was. As soon as I stopped, though, it finally realized that something wasn't quite right, and set off into the field by the road. The bewildered lamb led me a merry chase until I managed to catch it and carry it back up the road to where its mother was trying to puzzle out where junior had disappeared.

Sheep and lambs were a constant element wherever I went in the Highlands, usually filling fields at the roadside, but all too often filling the road as well. With disturbing frequency I would come around a turn or off a hill only to find lambs and sheep blocking the way ahead. The animals would immediately begin evasive tactics, which usually meant zig-zagging frantically, generally right in front of where I was trying to go.

Pedaling and walking up to the summit of an 1100-foot pass just about did my knee in, but luckily from the top of the pass it was a nice downhill ride to Loch Broom. Once down to sea level, I managed a very slow pace back up the loch to Ullapool. By the end, when my knee was *really* hurting, I felt ridiculous in the extreme, walking the bike on the flat as well as up even the gentlest slopes, my walk quite slow and gimpy-legged. Without doubt, I decided, the following day would be devoted to rest.

It was nice to be back in the Ullapool hostel, out of the wind, able to sit down with no need to go anywhere. I had covered 225 miles over quite hilly country during the past few days of travel, and with the difficulties experienced with Braw Handsel, it perhaps was too much for an amateur cyclist. (I tried to repress the thought that cyclists often cover that much distance, and more, in races lasting a single day.)

To celebrate the prospect of a day of rest, I created an evening meal of canned meat, corn, bread, butter and jelly, Frosties and one Amazin Raisin bar. While I prepared all this, I suggested to the other diners in the hostel kitchen that we play musical meals, each preparing their dinner, setting it on the table, and then scrambling about, enjoying whatever meal we found in front of us. For some reason they all inspected my culinary efforts and decided not to play.

Nine
On to Cape Wrath

A day of rest in Ullapool rejuvenated my enthusiasm—as well as my knee. My excitement rose at the prospect of pushing on to Scotland's northwest county, oddly named Sutherland-shire. The name seems less odd when one learns that it comes not from the Scots, but from Norsemen, who overran the area in the 11th century and held it for nearly 100 years. From their viewpoint, it was a southerly extension of their power.

My aim in heading north through Sutherland was to ride out to Cape Wrath, the most remote point of Scotland extending in this direction. And who could possibly resist visiting a place with a name like that, although I believe it is far less exciting when translated back into its original Norse. Cape Wrath means "turning point" in that language, the point where the Norsemen turned their ships south to reach the Scottish islands they also held.

Sutherland is a very barren county, rocky and mountainous in the south, more gently sloping to the north, the most sparsely populated of any in Scotland. This last characteristic was greatly advanced by the notorious Highland Clearances that saw some 15,000 peasants forcibly removed from their homes here, to make way for the introduction of the more profitable Cheviot sheep. After the brutal suppression of the Jacobite Highlanders, following their defeat at Culloden, the clan chiefs discovered that the number of armed men they could put on the field, which had been the measure of their power and wealth, now meant nothing. Many of the chiefs were quick to take steps to change their men to sheepherders in search of greater incomes, hence the infamous Clearances.

The early morning's bright sun slipped behind dark clouds before noon,

The rain cloud ambushed me as I sped down the steep hill to the Kylesku ferry across Loch a Chairn Bhain.

and I was met by gusting winds as I crossed the line into Sutherland, forcing me to wonder what such a welcome might augur for my journey through this county. The winds were so strong that I had to pedal in low gear downhill again, and on flat ground I had to walk Braw Handsel. When the gusts weren't coming from the front, they lashed at me from the side. Several times, riding down a slope in the protection of banks by the road, I would leave them only to feel that my wheels were about to be blown out from under me. Some fun.

I was anxious to reach the intersection town of Ledmore, some 15 miles north of Ullapool, to get out of the wind for at least a brief rest. It was a little disappointing to discover that this particular metropolis consisted of one phone booth. But, then, beggars can't be choosers, so I settled down in the lee side of this structure to consume a candy bar and to rest my wind-blown body and nerves.

I was happily chomping away when I looked up and saw another cyclist heading my way, south on the road that was going to carry me north. This short, pleasant, bristle-mustachioed young man ruined or at least began to ruin what might otherwise have been a nice day.

After the usual preliminary hellos, greetings and other introductory remarks, coupled with some polite but spirited shuffling for position out of the wind behind the phone box, I stupidly asked how far he normally went in a day.

"Well, that depends," he replied.

"Well, what's your furthest?" I persisted.

"Oh, this trip, about 140 miles," he answered. "I don't want to push it too much—only about 100 miles each day."

Damnation, who was this fiend? It was going to take me more than two traveling days to cover the same distance, with a day of rest thrown in between.

Sensing the impact his words had made, this maniac was kind enough to allow as how he had "done a little racing in the past." He also mentioned that in one 24-hour race he had logged over 300 miles. (Ye gods, he could take my whole trip so far in four days at that rate.)

Realizing that I still was not recovering very well, he also admitted, "My friends do think me a bit daft" and went on to point out that I alone weighed more than he, his cycle and all his equipment combined, implying either that I put too much weight on Braw Handsel and unavoidably slowed it down, or else that I had better go on a severe diet if I meant to do any serious cycling. He was a nice enough fellow, even if he was completely unaware of how devastating his words and statistics were to a fledgling cyclist who was happy with 20 or 30 miles a day, overjoyed with 40 or 50, in a state of shock each time 60 miles were managed. (Actually, in 53 traveling days, I averaged just under 40 miles per day.) We talked on for a while, then parted company. He flew away before the wind while I struggled toward the north, pushing directly into the blast.

The wind finally veered a few miles later and, at my back for a change, sent me sailing down a long hill to the Inchnadamph Hotel at the head of Loch Assynt. This structure seemed empty and closed, quite in keeping with the lonely country stretching all around, so I headed on up the loch to inspect the ruins of Ardvreck Castle, standing in picturesque splendor on the shore of the loch.

The sun came out from behind the clouds, and I rather cockily thought how nice it was to have it on call for a photo. This cockiness increased as I climbed out of the valley and looked back to see the mother and father of all black rain clouds creeping over the hills to the south, like a giant spider bent on devouring everything in its path.

"'Ha," I thought, "look at that rain back there. I'd be wet through if my timing were a little off, but here I am, slipping away, dry as can be." The cloud, far smarter than I, sent a flanking tendril around behind the hills to my right, and ambushed me as I sped down the steep hill leading to the Kylesku Ferry across Loch a Chairn Bhain.

"Oh, well, this isn't too bad," I thought, with persistent rashness, as the first sprinkles hit me. I should have known that those initial drops

86

were merely ranging salvos. Once it had me nicely lined up, that cloud let loose with every ounce of water it had, all squarely on target. I felt I'd been firehosed.

The wind drove the rain at me from all directions, and the brakes were useless on the wet tire rims as I flew downhill and nearly off the dock at the bottom. Desperate to get out of the nearly solid water, I flung a poncho over Braw Handsel and ran inside the small hotel hunched on the rocks just above the ferry landing, where I wrapped my shivering self around the nearest floor heater. Of course, 10 minutes later the sun was shining, mocking my drenched condition.

The break in the rain lasted only a few minutes, and then a steady drizzle set in. The ferry remained a long while on the other side of the narrow loch, but at last it came back and a few minutes later I hurried back off the ferry on the other side.

For some reason, this just wasn't my day. But I couldn't seem to learn. I was pedaling along, a mile or so from the ferry, and the thought entered my mind, "Hey, even with the rain, this isn't all that bad."

Presto, instant flat tire.

So once again it was into the tube-changing routine at which I was beginning to be pretty good. Over went the bike, off came the tire, then I sat down (rather wet) and wrestled the tire off the rim. Out came the tube. There was a tiny hole in the side of the tube, at the end of what looked like a long scratch. Now what in the world could cause something like that? In went a new tube, and there followed a great battle to get the wet tire back onto the wet rim, and then the wheel went back onto the bike. As I turned Braw Handsel back over, I felt a great wave of distrust sweep over me. How in the world could I be having flat tires for no reason whatsoever? And was that a wicked laugh coming from somewhere nearby?

I was wet and cold now, and my mood deteriorated even further while walking Braw Handsel over some three miles of road construction because I was not about to risk the tires on such a rough surface. Things did not improve much when I reached the small, rambling town of Scourie. A woman at the top of the hill before the town was reluctant to take a guest in her B&B, forcing me to go down into the town beyond. There, however, no other B&Bs were even open for business. So I phoned back to the place on the hill, and yes, now she would take me. But why not in the first place, I thought as I pushed Braw Handsel back up the hill?

Once inside the woman's home, however, I began to feel better. I had become quite chilled, so the heater in her front room was very welcome, as were the tea and biscuits she unexpectedly brought in. Before the sun set,

Alison Leach was happy and content only when she ventured out onto the farthest point of Cape Wrath.

it lit up the banks of clouds sitting on the hills around Scourie and turned the little town to gold, looking as though no drop of rain had ever fallen there. I patched the punctured tube, and wondered warily if I might eventually wish I had picked up more spares in Kyleakin.

The next morning offered the start of a beautiful, clear day. I set off, after pumping up the rear wheel and re-centering it, but I found that I just couldn't enjoy the morning. I was worrying too much over what Braw Handsel might do to me next.

Going down a shallow hill just three or four miles beyond Scourie, the rear tire seemed low again. I stopped and pumped it up, only to have it go completely flat while I was pumping away at it.

Damn.

It is nice and warm, I tried to rationalize, and one really has to expect these little setbacks now and then. So I turned over the cycle and arranged myself comfortably on the turf lining the road. Off came the wheel, out came yesterday's new tube, and there was the same hole at the end of a long scratch running along the side of the tube. A tiny pebble inside the tire, perhaps? But I found nothing. I patched the new tube, and replaced it with the other one I had patched the night before. Then came the tiresome routine of getting the tire back onto the rim, fitting the wheel back onto the bike, tightening it and turning the whole thing back over again. It is surprising how dirty and greasy you can get doing this.

I pedaled off 40 minutes after I stopped, expecting real trouble at any moment, but none came. It proved to be a very pleasant ride on to Durness, on Scotland's north coast. The land became far more level, looking less like a barren, jumbled rock pile, and on the last seven miles into Durness, the gods of fate or whatever offered up the best biking of the entire trip. I found myself, after a long but gradual climb, looking down an almost straight road that ran downhill nearly all the way to the little village by the sea. Overjoyed, hoping that I could get far down that beautiful ramp before the next problem with Braw Handsel developed, I set off. A great sweep of landscape opened out in a shallow valley to my right, and the ocean stretched blue to the horizon ahead. What a beautiful ride that was. Nothing went wrong. The hill was just steep enough to keep the cycle gliding nicely, but not so steep that things ever got out of control.

In Durness I learned the name of the ferryman who would take Braw Handsel and me across the Kyle of Durness in his small, open boat. (There is no direct road to Cape Wrath.) John Muir said that it would have to wait until the following day, however, so I looked around Durness for my next B&B, as the hostel there was still closed.

I ended up staying in a B&B run by a great rollicking figure of a woman. She named her price for bed, breakfast and the dinner for which I was hungry. When I winced at the total, she stepped closer, named a much nicer figure, but warned me not to let her other guests know of it. How very nice.

My hostess was a constant laugher who assumed massive mock outrage when I mentioned a desire to put Braw Handsel in her front entryway. She was also a devil over a pair of newlyweds who were trying to spend the night without anyone knowing of their recent marriage. The hostess went around the next morning and happily explained to everyone how the couple had pushed their twin beds together for the night. Her evening meal of soup, several helpings of meat and potatoes, salad and a delicious dessert of ice cream and cake and hot pudding sealed my admiration for this essential woman beyond any doubt.

I was somewhat doubtful over the trip I planned to Cape Wrath the following day, wondering if the cursed tire on Braw Handsel would give me further trouble. After all, there were no additional fresh tubes to insert, and Durness certainly was no source for them. (The little town had only two or three stores, each with a bare minimum of goods, which did not include Dunlop high-pressure bike inner tubes.) I consoled myself with the thought that the ride out to the Cape Wrath lighthouse was only 11 miles in length once I crossed the kyle, and that in the last extreme I could walk such a distance if I had to.

The next morning I woke to the sound of pouring rain, and thought, "Right, there goes Cape Wrath." By the time breakfast was done, however, the sky was blue again and the day seemed quite acceptable for such an excursion.

Waiting at the edge of the Kyle of Durness for Mr. Muir to travel the several hundred yards from the other side, I was surprised to see another cyclist, this one a girl in rolled-up jeans, come pedaling out to the end of the road where I sat. In a brief but spirited burst of conversation I learned that her name was Alison Leach, that she was an M.D., that she had worked for several years abroad in such far-flung places as New Zealand, South Africa and America, that she was English but lived and practiced in Scotland now and that she was going to Cape Wrath as well. This was welcome company indeed.

Mr. Muir came bobbing across the rough waves of the kyle, his route directed from the bow of the small, open boat by his equally small but very officious dog, Patch. It was a bouncy, wet ride across, but I craftily took a seat in the middle of the boat, leaving Alison the far wetter rear seat. She bore her dousing stoically, though, showing all the virtues the British are often noted for. Once across, we pushed our bikes uphill from the cement ramp, and began our ride to Cape Wrath. The road was narrow and very rough, quite different from what I would like to have had under my now-doubtful tires.

Alison, riding a clunky old bike that still seemed to serve the purpose, proved to be faster going down hills. Her great soft tires were impervious to any damage, while I often walked my cycle to prevent anything happening to mine. I was faster going uphill, though, and as a result the ride to the lighthouse involved one of us passing the other constantly, carrying on a running conversation as we passed by. We talked about a great number of things, and (as was the case with the Australians by the Falls of Measach), we both seemed to enjoy our mutual enthusiasm for any sort of travel around the world.

Cape Wrath is a very empty sort of place. The land was covered by heather, undulating rather sharply, seldom giving us any extensive field of view. It was nice, though, particularly when we came to little streams or the odd inlet of the ocean, which lent contrast to the barren nature of the land.

At last, we came to the bulky Cape Wrath lighthouse. A sign there said that no one should enter at that hour. We walked in anyway, not about to go back after coming this far. Several people saw us, but as they made no reaction, we walked on through the lighthouse compound and onto the rocks beyond. This is the very end of Scotland in this direction, next stop Iceland. At this point we were standing nearly 400 feet above the crashing waves directly below, while flights of gulls wheeled and turned among the rough rocks below us. Yet Alison was happy and content only when she ventured out onto the farthest point she could reach, commenting that something in her always made her act that way. I left those crumbling edges to her, and contented myself with absorbing the scene, enjoying the ocean working against the cliffs below, the Scottish mainland stretching away east and south from this point.

It was well worth the ride out, I thought, and Alison agreed.

I mentioned to her that there was a cycling magazine in London (appropriately named *Cycling*), which gave some sort of award to each cyclist who made the ride out to Cape Wrath, and grandly said that I would submit our names. Now both Alison and I have an impressive certificate, complete with a photo of a determined cyclist, that announces to all the world the following:

> "This is to certify that Eugene Cantin/Alison Leach has been elected a member of the Cape Wrath Fellowship he/she having during the year 1974 ridden a bicycle from Keoldale Ferry, Durness, to Cape Wrath Lighthouse, at the north-western extremity of the Scottish mainland."

What a nice thing to receive, unexpectedly. What an honor. Of course, by now the Cape Wrath Fellowship must number in the thousands, but that doesn't really matter. In any case, Alison and I were the only ones to manage this heroic feat on May 13th.

We knew nothing of having earned this great award at the time. We simply sat on the rocky point awhile, then turned around and rode back to the ferry. There the waves on the channel had become far larger than when we first came across, and the mighty Captain Patch had his work cut out getting us across. He managed it, though, with the aid of his master, Mr. Muir. As we approached land, we were greeted by the sound of bagpipes drifting down from the grassy fields above us. A man was there, practicing I suppose, and the sound of the pipes was perfect in such a setting.

John Muir said that he would not take a load of summer visitors out on the channel the way it was when we crossed, and we were quite happy to reach the other side without having to try cycling underwater. We said good-bye to Mr. Muir and the mighty Patch, then pedaled our way back to Durness, under a ceiling of black and threatening clouds.

It had been an enjoyable day spent with Alison, riding cycles across the empty lands of Cape Wrath, and I was sorry it was ending. We were both heading in opposite directions the following day, however, so I said that I would contact her if I came near Muir of Ord on my way south, and we bade each other good-bye. It had been a very pleasant day.

Back at the B&B, I found my hostess in a bantering mood. So we went at it for an hour before dinner, each complaining of the other's vast social faults and other shortcomings, not to mention our differing opinions on Braw Handsel's excellence and proper claim to a space inside the house. Of course, I was fighting to keep Braw Handsel happy, glad that my cycle had managed to get through this day without throwing further difficulties my way. Perhaps I should have slept in the entryway myself, however, and given Braw Handsel the room upstairs. Unfortunately, that thought didn't occur to me at the time.

Ten
On to the Orkneys

I left the warm hospitality of the Scourie B&B a little after 9 the next morning, venturing out into a clear, wonderfully bright day. The rain had poured 20 minutes earlier and 20 minutes before that, it was clear and beautiful. You never have to worry about getting bored with the same old sort of weather all day long in Scotland.

I pedaled east from Durness, along the coast, then turned south to make the long loop around Loch Eriboll. This proved to be a lovely loch, its blue waters set in a great sweep of hills, here and there a touch of green from stands of trees, and overhead a nearly cloudless sky. It was so beautiful that I couldn't resist stopping a little way down its shore to take a photo of a house sheltered under several large trees.

As I clicked the shutter, Braw Handsel's rear tire went flat.

So okay, it is a nice day, and we will remain calm. The bike goes over, off comes the wheel, off comes the tire, out comes the tube, I patch it, put it back, put the tire back on the rim, the wheel back on the bike and turn everything over again. And we are off.

Except that the tire immediately went flat again.

Well, all right, you can't always expect to have things the way you want them, now can you? So over goes the bike, off comes the wheel, off comes the tire, out comes the tube, I put in the other patched tube, put the tire back on the rim, put the wheel back on the bike and turn everything over again. And this time it works. See, things aren't so bad.

I pedaled down one side of the loch, rounded its lower end, and headed back up the other side. On a hill there, where I had to push the bike, there was a man cutting out sections of heather he intended to use for roofing on a house he was building. We talked awhile, stopping to wave to two girls who putt-putted by on a motor scooter, their helmets incongruous with the slow speed their machine made up the hill. Shortly after they passed I said good-bye to the man and walked Braw Handsel on up the hill.

On the top, the rear tire went flat.

Well, now, Job certainly had a worse time than this, now didn't he? And after all, it is a nice day, isn't it? So let's get on with fixing this little problem that certainly isn't going to make us angry. Over goes the bike, off comes the wheel, off comes the tire, out comes the cursed tube whose cursed patch isn't holding, in goes the other tube, on goes the tire, back goes the wheel onto the bike and the whole thing goes right side up. I get on and we are off.

Except the rear tire goes flat again.

"@**!?//!!**+@!!! Braw Handsel, I hate you."

Calmly, calmly. We are, after all, out in the middle of nowhere, no cars at all have passed all morning, this is your only means of transportation you currently are cursing and it would be better if you tried to fix it instead.

Over goes the bike. Off comes the wheel. Off comes the tire. Out comes the tube. Patch it once more (it is beginning to look like a patchwork quilt in rubber). Put the tube back in the tire. Put the tire back on the rim. Put the wheel back on the bike and turn the bike over.

The wheel goes flat.

How about a dance to the joys of spring performed on the cursed frame of this infinitely cursed cycle, which so obstinately refuses to act like a cycle, and cycle? How about a contest to see how far I can throw this cursed cycle into the waters of cursed Loch Eriboll? How about an experiment to see how long it takes to set a certain cursed cycle afire?

Luckily all of these thoughts remained thoughts. I was left standing by the beautiful loch, a cycle resting against my side, its rear wheel exceedingly flat. I was some 16 miles from Durness to my rear, a good 20 miles from the next town of any size, Tongue, in front of me. And oh, yes, now the sky was clouding up again, with an excellent promise of rain.

I pushed toward Tongue, trying to ignore the squelching sounds from Braw Handsel's incapacitated rear wheel. I didn't really know much about cycles, even now, but even I knew that this treatment could not be in the bike's best interests. Still, there was nothing else to do. As I went, I grew more and more amazed at just how much work it is to push a bike with a flat tire, especially when it is loaded down with 35 pounds of equipment. Braw Handsel was pushed as easily as a load of bricks.

I had covered five or six miles when I finally heard a vehicle on the road behind me. I turned, and discovered that a large camping van was coming slowly up the road behind me. There was enough time to collect my thoughts, and those thoughts said loud and clear to try and catch a ride to Tongue. So I waved, and luckily the van stopped for me—I was standing in the middle of the road, Braw Handsel turned across it in front of me. I mean, I really wanted that ride by now.

The couple inside could not have been a better pair to seek help from than if I had conjured them up myself, as perhaps I had. They were young, Australian, and making only a two-year trip around the world. I explained what the problem was, and asked very directly if they would take me to Tongue.

They said, "Sure, hop in."

We reached Tongue, which appeared to be a spot where a fully equipped bike shop would be very unlikely. Without such a shop, I foresaw a bus ride to Thurso, then probably a train ride south to Inverness. I decided to press my luck.

"Are you two by any chance going on to Thurso?" I asked.

"Well, yes, we do hope to get there tonight," the young man replied.

"Will you take me?" I added.

And again this delightful young couple made themselves even more delightful by saying, "yes."

So I helped pay for gas, and we were off across the top of Scotland, almost from corner to corner.

I did not like the idea of riding in the van over land I had planned to cross by cycling. It seemed to be a form of cheating, a sort of invalidation of my efforts around Scotland by cycle. Up until now I had covered a closed circuit by bike, at least on the mainland. Now, unless I somehow came back to Loch Eriboll and retraced the route of the van, there would be a great gap in my course around Scotland, which I didn't like.

Surprisingly quick, at least for someone who had been riding for weeks only as fast as a cycle might carry him, we were in Thurso. Thurso is the largest town (pop. more than 8000) in Caithness-shire. Caithness is Scotland's most northeasterly mainland county, but in nature it is far more similar to the Lowlands of Scotland than to the Highland counties that surround it. Its surface is composed of green and brown plowed fields instead of the barren heather, rock and open pasturage so prevalent in all the Western Highlands I had passed through. In addition, Thurso was easily the largest city I encountered since Glasgow. Its size came as a shock as it was so totally unexpected. Also, where so many of the little towns I had passed through during the past few weeks seemed set in at least the 19th century, if not the 16th, Thurso seemed to be more in the 21st. Just a few miles west, at Dounreay, stands Scotland's oldest industrial atomic energy plant, of all things, very conspicuous under its 135-foot sphere, with a new installation going up beside the old.

As we came over the hill and found Thurso spread out below us, I felt a surge of hope well up in me, that perhaps such a town might have a bike shop all its own, and maybe even a laundromat and a good restaurant. Finding these items there would help offset my horror at being back on roads filled with honking cars and trucks whizzing past. Such conveniences also would help dissipate my regret at having left behind the beautifully rugged scenery of the West, to which I had grown quite happily accustomed.

We reached Thurso at five that evening, and as friendly as the Aussie couple were, they also were quite ready to part from their unexpected passenger and go on about their trip—in this case heading on to John O'Groats at Land's End. I was deposited rather rapidly on a street corner in the middle of Thurso, feeling a bad case of culture shock sweep over me at all the hustle and bustle, wondering how in the world I could encompass the silence of Loch Eriboll and the noise here all in one day.

I found a very inexpensive B&B a few blocks from where I was let out, checked in, then asked if there just happened to be any cycle shops in town.

"Why, yes, there are two," answered the proprietor. "If you hurry, they should still be open."

One of the shops was closed, and looked too small to suit my needs, but the other one was open, and it was exactly perfect. The shop was run by a Mr. Hughes, a short, gruff man who proved to be fanatically interested in repairing cycles properly, and extremely gentle and helpful where obviously amateur cyclists were concerned. He heard my story, and after examining the wheel, he thought that it might be too deep for the tube. He decreased the wheel's inner size by putting a second tape around the rim inside the tube, and installed a new tube to replace my oft-patched one.

I purchased another spare, and left the shop ready to travel again. How lucky can one be? I had felt certain of spending at least two days of aggravation getting to Inverness and back. However, here I was, ready to roll the same day that Braw Handsel decided to fall apart. Walking back to the B&B I almost could hear Braw Handsel muttering, "Curses."

Instead of being days behind the vague schedule I had in my mind for each section of the trip, I now seemed to be a day or two ahead. This development seemed unbelievable, considering that just three or four hours before, I had been pushing Braw Handsel through the middle of nowhere.

I was surprised at breakfast the next morning to find the two girls who passed me on their single motorcycle the day before, just before Braw Handsel broke down for the last time. They were jaunting through Scot-

The ferry curved around toward the port of Stromness, on Mainland in the Orkneys.

land during their holidays, trying to see as much as they could. Both were social workers in Aberdeen, and as one was perky and cute, and both were pleasant to talk to, I asked for their address in Aberdeen before they tore off for the day's run out to Land's End and on toward the south. They gave it to me, saying that I should be sure to stop and see them if I reached their city, and off they went in a cloud of noxious fumes.

I spent the morning making use of the amenities a town the size of Thurso offers a traveler, going to the post office and bank, getting needed shoelaces and even a haircut—my first in three months. Then it was time to go.

My destination from Thurso was the main island of the Orkneys, named somewhat egocentrically, Mainland. This island was located due north of Thurso, across 18 miles of open sea, called the Pentland Firth. I pedaled the short distance from Thurso to Scrabster, and caught the ferry just before it left at 1 o'clock.

Because of the unfortunate events on my last ferry ride from Stornoway to Ullapool, and because several people had happily told me that the Pentland Firth made the Minch look like a placid mill pond, I was ready for the worst. I swore that I would stay at the railing no matter how rough the going got—breathing that fresh sea air.

In fact, it proved to be a beautiful 2½-hour ride. The wind blew fairly hard, the sea air felt comfortably bracing and the sun seemed quite warm as long as you were out of the wind. It was a clear day, and I always had something to occupy my eyes. Dunnet Head, the most northerly point of the Scottish mainland, stood to the right as we left the Thurso harbor. The massive island of Hoy, and beyond this, Mainland, rose slowly over the ocean's horizon, all the while innumerable gulls performed complicated maneuvers for our enjoyment.

The ferry route from Scrabster headed almost straight north, up the left side of Hoy, then curved around toward the port of Stromness, on Mainland. On the way, the ferry runs right by the Old Man of Hoy, which I was anxious to see. The Old Man is a rock pillar 450 feet high, the highest in Britain, I believe, standing free from the cliffs of Hoy behind, cut away from them by the action of wind and water over the ages. It is doomed to eventual decay and collapse, but for now it stands as a tribute to the amazing artistic possibilities of nature, much like Fingal's Cave on Staffa. As we passed, I snapped photos, enjoying the golds and reds striating the rocky pillar and cliffs behind, and amazed by the number of birds that swooped and swirled around this lonely pillar.

Between Hoy and the curve of Mainland and several other, small islands, there lay a large body of open, placid-looking water, Scapa Flow. During World War I this was the main base of the British Grand Fleet. In 1918 Scapa Flow became the site where most of the German Fleet—70 ships, including 10 battleships and numerous cruisers and destroyers, was held. On June 21, 1919, almost all of these ships were scuttled or run aground by their skeleton German crews, in a final act of resistance.

Since then phenomenal efforts at scrap salvage have raised many of these ships up off the bottom. Still, it was strange to look out over this bay, as we approached Stromness, and know that despite numerous salvage efforts, dozens of ships still lie hidden under those still waters.

Scapa Flow's naval history did not end with the sinking of the German Fleet. In October of 1939 the Flow's thin defenses were pierced by a German submarine, which torpedoed and sank the Royal Oak, killing 833 men. At this, Churchill decided that something had to be done to improve the area's defenses. He ordered causeways to be built, linking Mainland with several smaller islands, preventing access to the Flow from the east. Later, these links were elevated to form a road so that today Mainland effectively extends clear down the east side of the Flow to a point south of Hoy.

Stromness proved a village of about 1500 people, unlike any other I saw in Scotland. Its single, narrow street, paved in large flagstones, snakes through the surrounding buildings that seem to hunch down around it to provide protection from the unending Orkney winds. (There is a golf course at the end of this street where all its flags are on springs, so the wind won't break them off!) The entire village is huddled at the base of a high granite hill, and looks as though it is hunkering down out of the blast.

If the 17 miles I rode from Callanish to Stornoway on Lewis were the longest 17 miles of the trip, then the 15 from Stromness to Kirkwall were certainly the longest 15, because of the wind. The wind beat directly into me, and the bike seemed to stand still no matter how hard I pedaled. At one point I found myself angling back and forth—the way a kid will do on a steep hill—in order to move forward on the perfectly flat, if not actually downhill, road.

I had stopped—I wasn't going anywhere against the wind anyway—beside a field with a number of cows that wandered over to look curiously at the silly man on the bike. I was just explaining to them that they looked pretty curious themselves, when there came a very strange, squelching, rippling noise from under me. I yanked my eyes around and down to see what was making it—something chewing on my rear tire, maybe?—and there was the new innertube oozing its way out from inside the tire, a great balloon of it appearing between the rim and outer tire.

Ye gods almighty, how could *that* be happening? Well, it couldn't, it was impossible, but by now there was no question about Braw Handsel's incredible ability to produce these complications. I leapt off the cycle and just managed to release the air valve in time to take enough pressure off the tube to keep it from blowing apart. Then I threw the bike over in a fury, ripped the wheel off and jammed the new tube back where it belonged, all the while I explained to Braw Handsel how grateful I was for this experience, and how much I looked forward to the next. My mood was not the best.

The tire went back onto the rim with suspicious ease, probably because of the tire breaking down from the five miles I had pushed the bike on it while the inner tube was flat the day before (it seemed like weeks ago). After the whole thing was retightened and upright again, I just rested against the fence, the cows solicitously mooing about on the other side, as I tried to get myself out of the blues.

It just didn't seem much fun, trying to take a cycle trip when your cycle continually seemed to sabotage your efforts. I just didn't think that other cyclists could possibly have to put up with anything like this each time they set off on a trip. Yet here I seemed to be spending all my time turning Braw Handsel upside down and fiddling with the rear wheel.

After consoling myself over the more positive aspect of the trip, I slowly activated myself and pedaled off from the cows, after bidding them good-bye. Fortunately, the wind actually did drop, or at least it shifted from in front of me to the side.

At last I found myself in Kirkwall, sheltered from the wind by the cement buildings. I was happy to have reached my destination, but still not in a very good mood, feeling nearly down and out from the pummeling from the wind and the psychic pummeling Braw Handsel was meting out with inexplicable wickedness.

While looking for a B&B I was amused to pass a single, quite large tree standing in the middle of the flagstone street. The tree looked like an alien visitor, set into a protected area of the street, between the rows of solid Kirkwall shops and buildings. After a short look, I found a B&B on a side street that would take me, and I was eager for the comfort it offered.

I was in a far better mood the following morning, the other side of the emotional coin once again coming up after a night's sleep. I had an early breakfast, then went into town to shop for food to carry with me, and wandered through the impressive ruin of the 13th century Bishop's Palace. Near it was another structure, of a later date, called the Earl's Palace. By the time I had seen both of these, the Kirkwall Cathedral was open. Finally I stopped by the oldest library in Scotland, founded 300 years ago. It is strange how very recent such a number looks, alongside 800-year-old buildings. Nonetheless, that library was established in 1674, long before the United States was a country.

In the library, I had looked over a large map of the archeological sites on Mainland, and from that had decided against swinging clear to the north, around the coast. Instead, a route that cut straight across Mainland, to a point north of Stromness, would allow me to see the Rennibister earth house, the Maeshowe, the Standing Stones of Stennes, the Ring of Brogar and Skara Brae. These offered as incredible an array of prehistoric human artifacts as one could hope to see in a single day.

I left Kirkwall, driven by the wind, and enjoyed the ride along the Bay of Firth, its blue waters making a nice contrast to the neat green fields at the shoreline. After four miles I turned off the main road, to walk the cycle down the dirt drive of a farm, looking for the Rennibister earth house that a sign said was here.

A man cleaning out a farm building directed me rather abruptly into the center of the farm buildings, where I found a hatch leading down into the ground. Once down this, I found myself in an oval chamber, the roof of which was four or five feet high, supported by stones serving as columns. It was basically an artificial cave under the ground. Investigators are puzzled as to the use intended for structures of this sort, which date from the Bronze Age. Were they homes, graineries or what? Their use, of course, is obvious to the truly acute observer: they are holes dug to allow the diggers some protection from the endless winds overhead. (In fact, I think this explanation serves for every artifact I saw on Mainland.)

I clambered back out, impressed with the nonchalance of the site, lying as it does nearly ignored in the middle of a functioning farmyard. Only a low fence and a small sign from the Scottish Historical Society marks its presence.

About 9½ miles from Kirkwall, after a pedal up a brief hill, I came to a field with a strange, dome-shaped mound hulking on one side of it. This was the Maeshowe, or Great Cairn.

Almost 4000 years ago, men who were moved by the death of a great prince or powerful cult leader came to this lonely, out-of-the-way spot to erect the most magnificently chambered cairn in Western Europe. No record remains as to whom the cairn was for, but the tomb's huge size and the detail of its construction reflect that person's importance in those distant times.

The central feature of the Maeshowe is the earth dome, 25 feet high and 115 feet in diameter, with an outer trench 45 feet wide and six feet deep surrounding it. Hidden within this mound of dirt and its green topping of grass is an amazing tomb of stone. It is reached through a 36-foot passageway, four feet high and three feet wide, lined with enormous slabs of stone more than 18 feet long. Once past these slabs, there is a central chamber almost 15 feet on a side and nearly as high, also built from gigantic megalithic blocks of stone. Four great piers of stone support the roof, which was corbelled, each slab projecting in toward the center as they piled up. Three small chambers or cells open off of this central chamber. Each cell was roughly five by six feet on a side and 3½ feet high, raised two feet above the level of the floor of the main chamber, and entered through openings roughly 2½ feet square. The bodies originally stored in the Maeshowe were entombed here.

The great impact of the Maeshowe lies in the incredible skill with which its stone components are fitted together, the awesome size of those components and their incredible age. The Great Cairn is almost entirely composed of megaliths weighing up to three tons, many of which have been carefully dressed by pick and chisel. In places they are so carefully aligned that the classic knife blade will not fit between them. Protected as the cairn is under its dome of earth, the inner chamber seems as fresh and new today as when it was built. I felt like a time traveler, making my way hunched over through the entrance way, rising up inside the central chamber and sweeping my eyes about it, where eyes first examined the excellence of the work 4000 years ago.

Seven stone huts, the remains of a Neolithic community from 1500 B.C., were exposed by a winter storm that swept a high dune known as Skara Brae.

As if to underscore how old this structure is, another facet of the Maeshowe may be mentioned. Its walls are covered by 24 runic inscriptions, which were carved into the stones on different occasions. Some of the runes indicate they were carved by Crusaders who broke into the cairn looking for treasure, and another set, dated January, 1153, mention that Earl Harold and his men were driven there by a snowstorm.

It is easy to picture the stolid Vikings standing about, a small fire lighting up the great slabs that protected them from the storm piling up snow in the entrance passageway. One or several men, bored by the lack of action, pulled out their knives and began scratching these messages into the stone. There is even a well-executed Viking dragon. We look at these carvings today, and they seem incredibly old, connected with the Vikings as they are. Yet when those men carved their messages, the Maeshowe had been standing there for almost 3000 years. Such antiquity is mind boggling, especially when coupled with the expertise shown in working such gigantic materials.

When I first arrived at this site, I found two men waiting about outside the locked gate guarding the entrance. A sign directed me to the farm across the road for the key, where I discovered that the farmwife would

102

show the tomb for a small fee. I went back to the entrance, where the two men were still waiting, and we began to chat. The two gentlemen proved to be both intelligent and interesting, their work offering a perfect contrast to the ancient tomb we were waiting to inspect.

Bill Cairns and Frank Howie were both neatly dressed, energetic men between 30 and 45, I would guess. They were in the Orkneys to gain information to advise Occidental Petroleum on the possible environmental impact of that company's planned oil depot on a tiny island in Scapa Flow. In effect, they admitted, they were the company's devil's advocates, telling the company on what points it might well be attacked by outside environmentalists. I didn't realize this at the time, but Mr. Cairns was the personable head of W.J. Cairns and Associates, an architectural company in Edinburgh, intent on expanding its interests into the new environmental field. Both men were quite excited about their work, pointing out how unique it was.

"The North Sea is the first natural resource treated from the start as limited," one of them explained, "and the first to be treated as carrying social implications. Five years ago it would have been merely an engineering problem, nothing more."

We went through the tomb, and as we left I asked both men to stand by the dome of earth that held it. I thought it made a provocative contrast to photograph oil men standing on a 4000-year-old Neolithic structure with Viking carvings on its inside walls. How strange and varied is the course of human history.

The three of us thanked our guide and walked back to the road, where Mr. Cairns invited me to join them for lunch at a restaurant a short distance down the road. This was located in a remade barn. Inside, to my great surprise, we found a restaurant and several shops that would have gone very well in San Francisco or Carmel. They were most certainly unlike anything I had seen in Scotland, let alone on the Orkney islands.

I had a superb meal of juice, curry, ice cream, fruit and coffee, spiced with one of the most interesting conversations I encountered in Scotland. We talked about architecture, a planned community I had seen in Washington, the course of the North Sea oil rush and the erie feelings we all had experienced in the Maeshowe. It was a very enjoyable meal, cut short only because my hosts had to hurry and catch a boat for another portion of their inspection. I was sorry to see them go, but very pleased to have met them. Mr. Howie even mentioned that he might be interested in Braw Handsel, once I was back in Edinburgh, and gave me his office address for contact.

After such a meal all the world outside looked bright and wonderful, a total reverse over my mood of the day before. I was in truly high spirits as I started on down the road, accelerated by the wind at my back. All I had to do to go speeding forward was just sit up straight, going even faster if I spread out my arms like sails.

Less than half a mile away I turned onto another road, and after a short distance came to the Standing Stones of Stenness. These stones were in two groups. Four stones are all that remain of the Circle of Stenness, with an 18-foot stone (the Watch Stone), standing by the road a short distance away. A little further on is the Ring of Brogar, with 27 smaller stones still standing. Originally, this ring was probably composed of some 60 stones. The ones that remain range in size from six to 15 feet in height and stand in a circle 340 feet across, surrounded by a ditch 30 feet wide and six feet deep.

The Stones of Stenness were impressive, but I did not find them anywhere near as awesome as the more unified stone arrangement at Callanish. Perhaps this reaction was because of the wind whipping at me as I tried to inspect them. (I'm still convinced that circles of stones like this were put up because of the wind. At least *one* of those stones would offer the builder protection no matter where the wind was coming from.)

Perhaps my lack of enthusiasm for the stones came from the "chunk-pinngg" sound that indicated another broken spoke as I rode up to the circle. Sensing how ebullient my mood was, trusty Braw Handsel saw fit to break spoke No. 10 for the trip. Just to show that he was not practicing favoritism, this one was on the outside of the wheel instead of against the gear block, where all the others had been.

My primary reaction to this new development was one of tired boredom with such continued antics. I was glad that I had decided not to make the long swing up around the north end of the island, and glad that I expected to be back in Thurso the following day, where the spoke could be fixed.

I simply ignored the break, and continued on my way, letting the wind push me six or eight miles on to Skara Brae, on Mainland's west coast.

In 1850 a winter storm of spectacular proportions lashed the Orkneys, and on the southern shore of the Bay of Skaill it stripped the grass and sand from a high dune known as Skara Brae *(everything* is named in Scotland) uncovering an archeologist's dream. Under the grass and sand, the storm exposed a cluster of seven stone huts, connected by covered alleyways, surrounded by the remains of a huge midden, or refuse heap. The huts were the remains of a Neolithic community from 1500 B.C., which was overwhelmed by some catastrophe—probably the sudden encroachment of sand driven by another great storm—its remains buried and preserved intact until they were discovered 3300 years later.

The huts of Skara Brae were built of flagstone blocks, which are still common on the nearby beach today. Shale served for the roofs and pavements, although the huts probably were not completely enclosed but rather had skins or turfs resting on whalebone crosspieces to complete their structure. The walls were often very thick—up to four feet in places.

The site must have appeared to be a low, large mound, and all of its features were probably aimed at providing the best possible protection from the wind and storms so common here. (Even visiting the site today, it was nice to slip into the walkways, down out of the wind.) Inside each hut the remains of a central fireplace framed by stones can be seen. There are small "pens" against the walls ringed by slabs that are thought to have been beds. These were probably filled with heather, and it is possible that they had canopies over them—there are stones at the ends of the beds that might correspond to bed posts.

It was interesting to wander about the site, because where the Maeshowe might correspond to one of our present day mausoleums or family burial edifices, this site would be the equivalent of a private home. It was easy to set people into each of the seven huts, and picture them at work or asleep within these structures. The archeologists believe that Skara Brae was entirely self-sufficient, as they have not found any sort of artifact here that obviously has come from somewhere else. It is thought that the inhabitants were essentially pastoral people, living on the products of their herds of animals, cattle and sheep.

In one description, mention is also made that the villagers of Skara Brae "made pottery of exceptionally poor quality." I like that, these poor people, lucky to be able to live at all in such a site, being put down for their poor pottery production 3400 years after the fact.

Finally the wind got to me, and I walked several hundred yards back to where I had left Braw Handsel waiting in a parking lot, and set off for Stromness. The wind was from dead ahead once again, and I ended walking most of the way back. It must have been quite hellish to live in such conditions all your days, for in a very short time I felt wind-blown and irritable. I stopped to ask a woman walking a dog for directions, as the roads bore no agreement to the lines on my map, and I made some comment about the wind.

"Well," she answered, smiling, "if there isn't a little wind, it just doesn't seem right." She also said they had received no snow in the Orkneys in the past three years, which amazed me.

I felt tired from the wind by the time I reached Stromness, and was happy to get a bed in a crowded little independent hostel right by the ferry wharf. I wandered about the town, and up onto the hill behind for a view of Hoy in the setting sun, and the history-filled waters of Scapa Flow. It all seemed so quiet from that hilltop. Yet men had struggled with themselves and their environment for 4000 years here, almost within sight of where I stood. What a shame that there is no way to gain a clear image of all that history, all its actors superimposed, so that we might see how different, or how much the same we are in comparison to these shades of the past.

Eleven
Heading South,
Inverness and Culloden

The ferry for Thurso left Stromness a little before 9 the next morning, in the strongest wind of the entire trip. At one point the wind blew my bike across half the rear deck, and it had enough force to cant the large ferry over toward one side and keep it that way for all the crossing. Luckily, though, the wind was as constant as it was fierce, so the ship traveled forward very smoothly despite the unusual sideways slant of its deck. None of the misadventures enjoyed on the Minch were repeated.

As soon as I touched shore at Scrabster I made for Thurso and the Hughes Cycle Shop, only to be told by Mrs. Hughes that her husband would not be in until that afternoon. As I wanted to be far gone from Thurso by that evening, my reaction was rather panicky.

"My God, when will he be back?"

"Oh, about 12:30," Mrs. Hughes answered, to my great relief.

I spent the hour or so I had to wait over lunch, then returned and was happy to find that Mr. Hughes was in. In fact, I was lucky to see him at all, as he hadn't expected to come back. Mr. Hughes greeted my presence in the gruff manner I think is typical of him, then turned his glare to Braw Handsel and the wheel that dared to make trouble after he had worked on it only three days before. Mr. Hughes replaced the broken spoke, and then he began to tune that wheel like a Stradivarius, spinning it on a jig with a metal edge that showed where the rim was out of true, and correcting it by tightening the spokes just so. The man worked over that wheel for at least an hour, until it was exactly to his satisfaction, and then he charged me only 50 p, about $1.25, for his work. What a relief, to have found such a savior in distant Thurso.

107

A mile of two after leaving Mr. and Mrs. Hughes and Thurso, I found myself struggling against a perfectly steady wind coming from absolutely dead ahead. Under such trying conditions, I decided to stop at a little cafe in a place called Castletown, five miles from Thurso, and study my map. I thought if I went to John O'Groats it would be another 16 miles straight into the wind, and then another 17 miles south to the town of Wick (where I hoped to pick up mail the next day), with the wind coming from the side. Or I could cut across, going 16 miles from Castletown directly to Wick, with the wind coming at me from a slight angle. When a friendly van driver came into the cafe and mentioned that the wind was hitting 40 to 50 miles an hour consistently, I knew I was going to take the shortcut.

The road to Wick was as flat as it could be. The grey, plowed fields of Caithness stretched out in all directions under a grey fog that enveloped the afternoon, sending down a fine mist over the countryside. Yet I had to pedal violently hard to move at all, often finding it easier just to walk the cycle. It ended up taking hours to cross the puny mileage I had to cover.

At last I reached Wick, a nice little town at the head of Wick Bay, facing the North Sea. Now, having arrived in Wick, I was definitely on the return route toward Edinburgh. With my arrival in Wick I had covered 1229 miles through Scotland, and had seen five of Scotland's major outlying islands: Mull, Skye, Harris, Lewis and Mainland. I could only hope that the return would prove as interesting and enjoyable as the outward route. And I could also hope—though I suspected it to be a forlorn hope—that Braw Handsel might finally cooperate and end his infernal breakdowns. Ten broken spokes, six flats, one escaping inner tube and one blown-up tube were really more than enough.

The next day I left Wick in a steady, substantial rain. It was an absolutely lousy day, but I found I enjoyed it. For once, I was forced to cycle properly, climbing aboard in Wick and pedaling continuously for the next hour and 40 minutes before getting off in Dunbeath for a meal of hot soup. I covered 22 miles with this effort, perhaps my best speed of the entire trip. I was amazed at how wet one can get riding a bike in a rainstorm, but I found it better to be active than still. At rest I could feel just how wet I really was.

After Dunbeath the rain became intermittent, and my steady course down the coast continued, as I labored to keep myself warm. The flat country of Caithness, with its fields and barns all laid out and hidden this day in the misting rain, slowly began to become a bit hillier. Then suddenly I was crossing the county line back into Sutherland, and back into Highland scenery as well.

108

The change was amazing. All the geometric fences were gone, all the flat fields replaced by rocky hills and heather, and sheep wandered about the open slopes. The eastern part of Sutherland seemed lusher and gentler than that in the west. As I headed south I was amazed by each succeeding mile, for they constantly became more and more pastoral. (Finally, around Inverness, the country seemed almost a physical embodiment of some purple-prosed pastoralist's most fecund fantasy.)

I stopped in Helmsdale, wondering if I shouldn't stay for the night, since it was really quite wet and cold by then. There was a hostel there, which was nicely empty. The old man who ran it, however, seemed so garrulous that I knew I would be pushing on farther.

The ride from Helmsdale to Brora, 11 miles down the coast, proved a very enjoyable end to the day anyway. Much of the ride seemed to be downhill. (Could there have been another wind at my back?) It started raining in earnest again as I approached Brora, and I knew I definitely had to stop.

Because of the rain this day, I really began to value the six largely dry weeks I had enjoyed so casually up till now. I had adjusted to today's rain fairly quickly by just putting up with it. However, I would never have been able to retain my interest in what was around me if such weather was constant, as many people had assured me it normally would be. Of course, I was being unduly cocky for thinking that I had "adjusted to the rain." This, my first day of prolonged rain, was also nearly windless. A rainy day that also was windy would be much more horrible indeed, and I could only hope not to face both conditions at once.

After a comfortable night at an excellent B&B in Brora, I loaded Braw Handsel up, said good-bye to the proprietoress and her two young children, Jim and Christopher Robin, and set off for a slow, enjoyable day's travel of only 31 miles.

My route carried me down the coast, past Dunrobin Castle, long-time home of the dukes of Sutherland, with a colossal statue of the first duke standing on the hill behind, visible for miles. Nearby there were the ruins of another, older "castle"—a broch by the road, its walls only four or five feet high. I continued on through Golspie, quiet and sleepy this Sunday morning, the only stir a line of men waiting for the Sunday *Times* at a news store.

The road ran up almost to the head of little Loch Fleet, crossing there on The Mound, then headed on across a low peninsula and up the length of Dornoch Firth to the town of Bonar Bridge. The country all about was a lovely, lush green, with plots of neon-yellow gorse here and there in contrast to the dark cloud overhead.

Inverness, a full-scale city often called the capital of the Highlands, has a history as deep and turbulent as any proper Scottish city could wish.

I crossed the Kyle of Sutherland on a quite substantial bridge at Bonar, then turned onto a back road to ride the four miles up to Scotland's ultimate youth hostel, Carbisdale Castle. Carbisdale Castle and the lands surrounding it were donated to the SYHA by Captain Harold Keith Salvesen. The castle is only 60 years old. An energetic 80-year-old man in Bonar Bridge explained that Dowager Sutherland built it to lord over the rest of her family, who had to pass under its walls whenever they rode the train. In any case, the castle is a great cavernous citadel of rooms, with a huge hall downstairs filled with sculptures of scantily cald white marble maidens crouching and standing in rather lascivious poses of alarm or anxiety. (They seem straight out of a Maxfield Parrish print.) It is great fun to wander about this place, venturing up the wide stairways to inspect its numerous rooms above.

Of course, the warden here assigned the few men who were here to beds in the same room, with at least 10 other men's dorms standing empty. (A switch later at night put me in charge of one of those emptier rooms.) The strangest thing about this great, rambling hostel is that the beds here are by far the narrowest of any I encountered in Scotland, like shelves propped up on legs. You either slept in a very still way, or else you ended up on the floor.

110

The next morning I went into Bonar Bridge, hoping to find some breakfast and a bank to cash a traveler's check. While waiting for the bank to open I fell into conversation with the 80-year-old man I mentioned earlier. He looked about 60, and in short order I knew he had been a sniper in WW I, and that he had served in the Canadian Navy in WW II. ("There's no fool like an old fool, so I volunteered.") He told me about the history of Carbisdale, which we could see dominating a low hill above the railroad tracks up the valley. He also wondered if Braw Handsel might be giving me trouble because he (Braw Handsel) was actually a she and therefore difficult, certainly a point worth considering. Finally I said good-bye, transacted my business with the bank, then pedaled back across the bridge.

Just beyond I passed two other cyclists heading north. As my trip progressed into May, I was to see more and more of them. Whenever I saw these cyclists, I had a deep sense of gratitude that I had made it through so much of Scotland during that unusual dry spell. I often found myself waving to them through misting rain, which I had not had to contend with for most of the first six weeks of my trip.

I pedaled along the lower side of Dornoch Firth, then pushed up to the high plateau that separates it from Cromarty Firth. Here the land reverted to typical Highland scenery, open land covered in heather and bare of any other distinguishing mark. I stopped at a little inn for a lunch of shepherd's pie, a perfectly timed pause as a violent rain squall went sweeping over. After the rain I headed on, enjoying the long run back down off the plateau, the road dropping back into even lusher lands than I had seen before, the fields and trees richly green, vibrant with life. Before racing down the hill I stopped and talked with a Canadian cyclist heading up the same hill. He mentioned that a cycling clubmate back home held the record for crossing Canada on a bike: 23 days. Yet another cycling statistic I'd just as soon forget.

Heading up a little back road from Evanton, a little town on Cromarty Firth, I found myself in a green tunnel of arching trees, a rustic, ruined gate standing open as though beckoning to a wonderland beyond. Such country as this seemed the proper home for some of the great children's stories that British authors have produced. The rockier Highlands to the west would seem the appropriate source for the more adult tales of blood and feud in Scottish history.

I went on to the fairly large town of Dingwall, and sat out a heavy spatter of rain there inside a pastry shop. Since it would be impolite to do otherwise, I had a pastry or two while I waited. Then on to Muir of Ord. I was forced back onto the main road, and did not like this development at all, pushed far to one side as I was by the constant flow of heavy traffic. At Muir of Ord I found a small B&B, then searched out where Dr. Leach said her home would be. There it was, and there she was, just pulling in from her day's ministrations to the sick of the area.

I find that I am very envious of Alison Leach. At 30, she is single and free, yet trained to practice a profession that makes her welcome anywhere she cares to travel and live in the world. As I mentioned when she first appeared in this chronicle, heading toward Cape Wrath, she has lived in such far-away places as New Zealand, South Africa and America, practicing her trade in each area, getting to know the people who live there far better than the casual traveler could ever hope to manage. She practices a highly respected profession, and one that is quite remunerative. Yet she has kept herself free from the usual snare of overwork that doctors always seem to fall into so that she is ready and able to consider pulling up stakes and trying another area if she wishes.

Alison was kind enough to be pleased at seeing me, waiting under the eaves of her house, out of the rain. We ran off to a store to get fresh supplies, then spent the evening talking and eating. Once again, as with the Australian couple I met at the Falls of Measach, there was a tremendous flow of enthusiasm between us, for each other's activities and pursuits. It was a very pleasant evening, as most such evenings are when you get a chance to talk at length with an intelligent person who is not only interesting, but also interested in your activities as well. It is like a feedback mechanism, and it made for a pleasant respite from the normal travel situation where you may meet people who seem as though they might be interesting, but you get no chance to become friends, at leisure. I was sorry to bid Alison goodnight and return to my boarding house.

The night before I did not know if I would leave, or simply take a daytrip in to Inverness and return to Muir of Ord for another night. This morning, feeling lazy, and liking the idea of traveling on an empty, lighter cycle, I decided on the latter course. I sat around reading, letting a brief rain pass by overhead, before setting off along a back road beside Beauly Firth, riding on the lower edge of what is known as the Black Isle, a wedge of extremely fertile land devoted to farms and pastures, formed by the Cromarty, Beauly and Moray Firths.

It was a beautiful day visually, dark clouds overhead in perfect contrast to the greens and blues of Beauly Firth, the fields full of cows nearby. I rode along very easily, and Braw Handsel seemed to like to travel without the 35 pounds of weight normally slung all about him, which I left at the B&B.

After a brief wait at the wharf at North Kessock, a ferry boat came

A cairn commemorates the defeated Highland clans at Culloden.

across and picked up several cars and me, and lugged us all across the mile-wide channel to Inverness.

Inverness is a full-scale city of almost 30,000 inhabitants, and is often called the capital of the Highlands. It sits astride the six-mile-long Ness River, which flows from Loch Ness to the sea. The city's history is as deep and turbulent as any proper Scottish city could possibly wish for. St. Columba of Iona is supposed to have visited a castle here A.D. 565 (MacBeth's castle, scene of Duncan's demise, was also located here.) The city has been taken and retaken many times in the arguments between the Scottish and English, and smaller imbroglios have also enlivened—and extinguished—life here over the years. I particularly like one succinct sentence found in the *Blue Guide:* "When Mary, Queen of Scots, visited the town in 1562 she was refused admission to the castle by the governor, but the castle surrendered the next day and the governor was hanged." Perhaps the job of governor was not the most desirable one in those long-ago days.

As is the case with so many large cities in Britain, Inverness is striking because of the way the green countryside seems to come right up to its borders, unlike so many of our cities that spread like a fungus out into the surrounding country, destroying it.

I wandered around the city, ducking out of the way of passing rain squalls, then rode on through it, heading for the long hill beyond on which lies Culloden Field, where on April 16, 1746, William the duke of Cumberland and his royal forces crushed the Highland army led by Prince Charles, and with it crushed all hope of the Stuarts ever regaining the throne of Britain.

The road leading out of Inverness was a heavily traveled main artery, and a very unpleasant one over which to ride. I was able to turn off onto a far smaller country lane after a mile, however, which climbed up onto a line of hills, with an excellent view out over the Moray Firth and back toward Inverness. Fields bordered the road, with great clumps of yellow gorse radiating everywhere. The road then passed through a wood, at the far side of which I found myself riding past the burial mounds and a high memorial cairn for the defeated Highland clans. A little further on there was a modern museum building containing explanations about the battle and the history that surrounded it, next to which was a single old farmhouse, roofed in thatch, that survived the battle. On beyond lay a boulder known as the Cumberland Stone, because the duke of Cumberland is said to have exhorted his troops while standing atop it. The memorial cairn was simply a round tower of stones with gorse growing about its base. The graves were at best low mounds with stones at one end signifying which clan lay buried where. Yet it is all very moving, the cairn and graves telling the visitor in the loudest possible terms, "Men fought and died here, right where you are standing, in bloody battle, for a cause most people cannot even name today."

The forces of King George II, led by his son the duke of Cumberland, were composed of more than 6000 foot and almost 2500 horse soldiers. Compared to the Jacobite forces, under the personal command of Prince Charles Stuart, the duke of Cumberland's troops were well-fed, well-trained, well-armed and well-led. In fact, this battle, between forces headed by cousins, was also between a trained "modern" army and the last feudal army ever mustered in Britain. The men standing with Prince Charles had come to his standard because their clan chiefs had commanded them to do so. The clan chiefs fought under Prince Charles' banner for a variety of reasons: preference for the line that had once ruled Scotland over the one from Germany; religion; or an inherent dislike for the clans who fought under the duke of Cumberland's banner.

Prince Charles had less then 5000 men to stand with him at Culloden. Many of the better informed among them thought this was the very last place they should choose to fight. The land was treeless in 1746, with turf that was firm enough for cavalry. The clansmen knew only one battle-tactic, the yelling battle charge, which allowed them to close with their main weapon, the broadsword. Yet at Culloden they formed a line approximately 400 to 600 yards away from the royal troops, and Prince Charles had them stand there for over half an hour while the royal artillery shelled them to bits. Then the clansmen charged, sleet and wind in their faces, over all that long distance, tiring themselves and giving ample opportunity for the three-line musket volleys of the enemy to cut them apart even further. It is estimated that between 1200 to 2000 of the clansmen died during these very brave and very futile attempts at war against an enemy that was to suffer practically no losses at all.

John Prebble, in his book *Culloden*, makes the following point about the background of sentiment against which the battle and its aftermath occured:

> "To an Englishman of the 18th century, and to most Lowland Scots, the Highlands of Scotland were a remote and unpleasant region peopled by barbarians who spoke an obscure tongue, who dressed in skins or bolts of particolored cloth, and who equated honor with cattle-stealing and murder. The savagery with which the Lowland Scots and English were to suppress the rebellion is partly explained by this belief, it being a common assumption among civilized men that brutality is pardonable when exercized upon those they consider to be uncivilized."

Driven by a thirst for vengence, by this misunderstanding of the Highlanders as beasts rather than men, by fear that they might somehow rise again, the victorious forces at Culloden took brutal control of Scotland. The duke of Cumberland, known as "Charming Billy" to his followers in the South, earned the name "Butcher" Cumberland for his acts in the North. His forces killed all the wounded they could find on the fields of Culloden, and even pursued and killed spectators of the battle clear into Inverness. Once the battle was over, they set about the determined suppression of all the Highlands. It was a harsh time, a brutal time, and it destroyed the Highland culture.

Twelve
Down the Long Valleys

M y route the next morning took me south from Muir of Ord, through Beauly, up Glen Convinth and back down to the town of Drumnadrochit near Loch Ness. The glen was extremely lush with lime and oak trees growing by the road and green fields running off over the bumpy little hills. Then the road climbed out onto the heathery Uplands, taking me back into the Western Highlands, before dropping steeply toward Loch Ness.

I stopped in Drumnadrochit to wait out the passage of a rain squall that came sweeping up the road, finding shelter over a bowl of soup in a little cafe. The rain passed, I mounted up and was just passing a nearby school when I heard that horrid sound: "Chunk-pinngg."

Broken spoke No. 11, rear wheel, against the gear block. Of course— thanks a lot, bike.

I sat by the road, glaring at the wounded cycle for a long while, trying to figure out what to do. I really did not want to pedal back to Inverness, the closest main town. I knew there was a small cycle shop in Fort William —my planned route down Loch Ness, and past Loch Lochy would bring me within nine or 10 miles of that town. I hoped the cycle would just hold together that long. If Fort William couldn't do the repairs, I could at least catch a train from there for Glasgow.

I pedaled down the length of Loch Ness, keeping an eye out for the monster, but saw nothing unusual in the loch's slate-grey waters. At the bottom end of the loch lies the small town of Fort Augustus, a pleasant-looking place whose stores unfortunately were closed for Wednesday early closing. I stayed there long enough to watch a ship going through a set of locks into the Caledonian Canal. The canal was constructed in the middle of the last century, effectively splitting Scotland in half and allowing ships

116

to pass through the heart of the country from Inverness to Fort William rather than making the stormy trip north, around Cape Wrath.

From Fort Augustus I went on down the Great Glen, and was almost to the little town of Invergarry when spoke No. 12 went. Right. With two spokes gone, the rear wheel was now definitely out of true, and it was obviously time for me to start walking the bike. Fort William was now out, but I decided to continue in that direction to reach the hostel at Loch Lochy just two or three miles down the road. On the way there I stopped long enough to take a look at Invergarry Castle, burned by "Butcher" Cumberland after his victory at Culloden, because it had housed Prince Charles on his flight from that disastrous affair.

A little farther on I passed one of the strangest monuments in all of Scotland. I was enjoying a portion of the road that ran under a roof of dripping trees that made the road a dark tunnel. I was almost past the peculiar stone monument before I realized the top of a short shaft had representations of seven heads, obviously severed from their bodies at the throat, with their hair tied in a knot and a knife stuck through it.

The monument is known as Tober-nan-ceann, or Well of the Heads. In the 17th century, a Clan Keppoch chief sent his two sons to France for their education, then died, leaving his seven brothers in charge of his affairs until his sons returned. When the two boys did return, however, the seven murdered them. The family bard in turn killed the brothers, and presented their heads to a higher chief, after washing them in a well here. With these dark deeds rattling about in my head I hurried on to the Loch Lochy hostel, and found it to be a large, rambling place with several outside barns and practically no one there to fill it up.

At Loch Lochy, writing in my diary, I realized with a shock that I had only about two weeks left for my trip through Scotland, as I had agreed to meet a friend in England after that time. I also realized that I had grown used to, and very much enjoyed, my seven-week tour thus far. With a good bike, I wondered if one couldn't enter into this sort of life endlessly, traveling gently along through enjoyable country, meeting the people, learning about the country's history. I realized just how much I was enjoying all this, even on this rainy day, even with Braw Handsel breaking down again. I knew perfectly well that a lot of this feeling involved the identity that I had created for myself over the past seven weeks, that of a long-distance (at least for me) cyclist, an identity that I realized I enjoyed, and that I would be sorry to give up. The positive rewards of a trip like this lay, for me, in the continuous stimulation it involved, elevating my senses to a level higher than just living a normal, stable life ever seems to do. This was borne out by the fact that I could easily relate exactly what I had done

117

and seen each unique day of the trip, while I couldn't possibly manage the same feat for any of the days that reel by so fast in "normal" life. A trip like this forced me to realize the joy of being active and alive each day, a wonderful thing. Two weeks left. Well, I could only hope that they would prove as enjoyable and rewarding as the past seven.

The next morning I was out on the road early, the rear wheel in one hand, the other hand thumbing for a ride. A van came by, and the driver gave me a ride all the way into the heart of Inverness. He had traveled all over the world, and currently was working as a painter and insurance salesman in Scotland. We talked all the way into Inverness, reaching town just as a heavy downpour came along. I was able to see a perfect demonstration of how people in Scotland cope with the weather. The streets were crowded, so I had plenty of people to observe. They defeated the downpour by completely ignoring it! There was no way to tell from their faces and reactions that it was anything but a perfectly nice, clear day. Amazing.

I went to one combination motorcycle-bike shop but the man there said that he had a terrible load of work and just couldn't deal with my

On a back road near Evanton, a rustic gate stood open as though beckoning; such country as this seemed the proper home for the great children's stories that British authors produced.

broken spoke today. He did suggest that I should try another shop several blocks away. I walked there, but this second shop was empty and closed.

A neighboring butcher said, "That lad is always out for coffee. Wait around, he'll be back."

I waited around in front of the locked door, and at last a bent old man —"that lad"—returned and opened the shop. As soon as I entered the door, wheel in hand, he barked, "Can't help you, I'm too busy, I'm retiring, I've done my duty for the bike community, can't help you, go away." Swell.

I walked back to the first shop, wondering if I would have to take the train to Elgin or some other large town nearby. The man there threw up his hands at my return and said, "I've got even more work now." Desperate, I told him that I had come all the way from Loch Lochy to get it fixed and couldn't he possibly help me? "Oh, all right," he answered. "Come back at four and I'll see if I can't help you out."

The man had fixed the wheel for me by my return at 4 o'clock, but he apologized for not having a pump to blow up the tire, or the proper spoke key for truing up the wheel by tightening the spokes. Fortunately, Mr. Hughes had equipped me with the proper tool in Thurso.

Back at the hostel later that evening, I was amazed at how scary I found trying to tighten those spokes. At any moment I expected to hear the ping of one breaking, which would be the sound of another day-long trip into Inverness. Happily, no ping came. I trued the wheel as best I could, straight enough for it to turn without scraping the frame.

The woman in charge of the hostel was in a dither this evening, as a group of hostel officials were to stay on their way to open a new hostel on Harris. Another girl and I were the only guests, and we speculated together on what sort of gnarled, tough, hoary but wise old outdoorspeople would appear. When the group finally did arrive they were something of a shock: it seemed likely that they had never been away from home before. They were older, certainly, but also fat and flabby, noisy and somewhat rude. One woman said she had never cooked in a hostel kitchen before, and how ever could she manage?

The wardeness scurried about, putting out tea and cakes for these people, while the girl and I—in effect these people's employers—sat one table away. We were offered nothing, as the officials feasted like kings. Fine hosteling spirit. (Perhaps my reaction would have been less severe if the cakes hadn't looked so good.)

These good people compounded their sins by very loudly *not* observing the rules for quiet after 11 p.m. What a fine example.

The next day was an excellent one. I had no difficulties, and covered as long a daily distance as any of the trip, 68 miles. All true and experienced bikers will, of course, laugh outright at such a measily distance, but I stand by it as my best, something of which to be proud.

I pedaled off down Loch Lochy under an ominous grey sky, which stayed with me throughout the day but held back all its rain. My route continued down the Great Glen from the Loch Lochy hostel, then swung in a curve toward the northeast climbing to an attitude of 850 feet before dropping gently down Glen Spey toward my destination, Aviemore.

There was a little town just where I was to swing back up toward the northeast, named Spean Bridge. I was sitting inside a small hotel there, having tea, when a little blue-eyed lady went by, pushing an old girls' cycle with a strange seat, more like a small stool top than a normal bike seat. A few minutes later, when I came back out, the same woman came up and asked if she might use my air pump for a moment. We talked while I pumped up her rear tire, and I found that she was one of the most memorable people I was to meet during the trip.

The little woman was German, and in her way one of the world's great bikers. She looked about 35 (in fact was 55), and her motto was, "I never go back, I always go forward." She would work a year, tending children in a playschool situation, then set off to cycle about the world. She had biked in Nepal, Japan, Australia, New Zealand and Europe, and now was touring Scotland for the first time. She said that English got her through all of her travels. She spoke this second tongue with a brisk crispness that seemed in keeping with her German background.

"I don't smoke or drink," she said. "That's how I keep young." She traveled only 20 to 30 miles each day, cycling along at a nice, easy, steady pace, usually from one hostel to another, spending a minimum of money. "I always pay cash," she stated. "If you are careful, you never have to spend too much." What a wonderful lady I thought, doing her traveling with such proud determination, covering continents on 30 miles a day.

Beyond Spean Bridge I began the slow climb up Glen Spean. By Loch Laggan I was passed by a car with a bike on a rack on top, whose driver pulled to the side to talk. He was also an enthusiastic cyclist, but his thing was to go only cross-country (cross-country on a bike?), using trails when he could, bounding over the countryside when he couldn't. My file of Facts I Don't Want To Know About had yet another addition.

The day went by easily, because I really didn't care how far I went or where I ended up. The endless days were those with a definite distance to be covered, which caused me to feel that the intervening country was in the way and something to be overcome. Today I just poked along, enjoy-

120

ing the climb up Glen Spean, then the slow drop down the increasingly beautiful valley of the River Spey, with the Cairngorm Mountains towering to my right. These granite peaks compose the largest mountain mass in Scotland, their 4000-foot peaks hidden under a coverlet of snow.

At Kingussie I wisely followed my rule about taking back roads, and turned off on one that paralleled the main route. I greatly enjoyed riding down the Spey Valley on this twisting lane, under sheltering trees and turning back toward Aviemore, for a night at my first grade one hostel. This was grade one largely because of a larger fee, free hot showers and its location. Unfortunately, the place was filled with a rather slovenly crowd, and as I had been spoiled by empty hostels almost everyplace else, I was quite put off by the place.

Aviemore was very strange, a pine-tree-country sort of town, with a huge cement winter sports complex of shops and hotels—like something snatched up out of Los Angeles or Las Vegas, plumped down in the middle of the sylvan countryside with predictable results. This place was populated by the strangest crowd of people imaginable, the sort of people you might expect to find on New York's 42nd Avenue, or perhaps in London's Soho District. Evidently these were kids dressed in their mail-order, pop-art, "real neat" clothing, attracted by an evening of "music" produced by some local overly amplified band. Really quite horrible, I thought, but then my opinion didn't seem to dampen their enjoyment of the place. Perhaps it is I who was wrong.

The next day was a slow, lazy one and quite enjoyable because of these characteristics. After waking up early and slipping out of the crowded dorm room, I had one breakfast of dry cereal, did my assigned chore, packed slowly, then rode into town for another breakfast of coffee and donuts, milk and an eclair. Thus energized, I climbed aboard Braw Handsel and began the day's journey on my beloved backroad, down the valley of the River Spey.

Throughout the journey until now, I largely had been traveling along coasts or cutting across river valleys. Now, with yesterday's climb up Glen Spean, and today's continuation of the run down Strathspey, I was traveling along the river valleys. On this day I hoped to reach Dufftown, and the next day I faced a long climb up to Tomintoul, Scotland's highest town. But after that I again would be running downhill, first to the River Dee and then along its banks clear to the North Sea at Aberdeen.

In all sports and athletic activities there are certain situations that make the practice of that sport almost perfect: the right snow for skiing, a windless sunny day for tennis, the right temperature of water for swimming.

And for cycling, I can think of no situation that can improve on mile after endless mile of gradual downhill, which allows you to travel at a good speed just sitting there, enjoying the passing countryside. I was really quite spoiled by these two days of downhill running. It was shocking just how hard it seemed to do even reasonable work afterwards, on ground that went up as well as down.

I left Aviemore under the usual cloudy sky, and found myself happily stopping for everything along the way—for photos, simply for looking at the changing view of the Cairngorms or just to enjoy the closer countryside without motion. To my side fishermen strode purposefully about, waist deep in the Spey, stalking their underwater quarry.

A sign invited me onto a still smaller road, to observe an osprey nesting site. At the end of a mile pedal I came to a lake, and a parking area filled with cars and people. Most of the latter were draped in binoculars and extremely long-range camera lenses, and we all trooped reverently to a viewing shelter, from which we were to observe the rare ospreys through mounted, high-powered field glasses. The nest seemed at least another quarter mile away, an osprey would have been a speck and I saw nothing, yet everyone else talked afterwards in deep tones of what a wonderful experience it had all been for them. There were some very good photos of ospreys diving into the nearby lake after fish, however, which I enjoyed very much.

Continuing on down the Spey, I found nothing in the way of a place to stop at Dalnashaugh or at Craigellachie, so I turned away from the River Spey at last, regretfully, and pedaled four miles up one of its tributaries—the Fiddich—to Dufftown, a small town of 1500 inhabitants who work mainly in the local distilling industry.

I stopped for a snack of so-called hamburger and chips at a little shop, and from there obtained directions for a local B&B. These directions led me several hundred yards down a road to the left of the town square, and there I found a place with a B&B sign. A lovely pregnant woman and a younger girl with a dog were at the door, and I asked if they had room for a guest. They seemed somewhat flustered, but finally the mother-to-be gave me a radiant smile and said certainly there was room, and that I should just ask their mother. I took Braw Handsel around to the rear of the house, where I found an older man. He also was certain a room was available, and that I might just as well go up to it. He also advised me to be sure to check with his wife.

I took Braw Handsel into a workroom at the back of the house, then went inside, where I met another young man, another girl, still another man coming out of an upstairs room as I was going up and still another girl by the room I was to have. All directed me onward to my room, and all suggested I check with Mother. It was the 21st birthday of one of the girls the following day, and the whole family had come to celebrate. I don't think I ever did see Mother.

Shakespeare was fond of omens and portents flitting by his characters before some fell event was to occur. For example, in *Julius Ceasar*, Calphurnia informs Ceasar:

> "A lioness hath whelped in the streets;
> And graves have yawn'd, and yielded up their dead;
> Fierce fiery warriors fight upon the clouds,
> In ranks and squadrons and right form of war, . . ."

And so on and so forth, all portents of Ceasar's impending death. I certainly do not wish to attempt any connection between what happened the following morning and matters of such importance as Ceasar's death. However, the events of the next morning did begin with a dream that turned out to be a fateful omen.

I never remember my dreams. So I was quite surprised to awake the next morning with an image fresh in my mind. It faded rapidly, but not before I had caught the faint outline of a bicycle with wheels melted so that the cycle's axles were almost on the ground. I have no idea what sort of dream could possibly have led to such an image, and as I got up I pushed the whole half-conscious matter out of my head. I went down to a good breakfast in the living room, then gathered up my things, thanked everyone profusely, wondered where Mother was, payed my bill and walked out to the workroom where Braw Handsel was left for the night. Braw Handsel's rear wheel was just as flat as in my dream, although the rim luckily had not seen fit to melt as well. Wonderful. Just the way to start the day.

Wearily I went into my normal routine. Over went the bike, off came the rear wheel, off came the tire and out came the tube. Throughout this I was completely unaware that Braw Handsel had entered into an entirely different realm of inspired devilishness. First, I reached into the saddle bags for the spare tube. Hmm, not in that bag, as usual, nor in the other. Come to think of it, I hadn't seen the box with the tube for some time. It's gone!

Now, logic of course says that I left that spare tube somewhere, as a result of one of my many loadings and unloadings since Thurso. However, by now I knew better than to accept logic: Braw Handsel obviously had spirited away that tube as part of his trickery. The cycle's joy appeared quite evident in the way his paint gleamed over my dismay at not having a tube with which to replace the flat one.

But Braw Handsel's genius this morning did not end here. Oh, no, the bike had become far more clever than that. Desperately I pumped up the tube, trying to find where the leak was. There was no leak! That devil bike had managed to get me to go through all the rescue motions needed to repair a tube that didn't need repairing! I couldn't believe it. I wasn't riding a cycle, I was riding a master of psychological warfare, who definitely was winning this war of nerves.

Braw Handsel's genius did not stop even there this day. The cycle set things up so that I would wonder and worry every foot of the way about its condition, and then carried me 68 miles, a distance equal to the longest managed on the entire trip! If any army could secure this "psycle" (sic.) and turn Braw Handsel against their enemies, they would conquer the world!

I left the B&B and rode into Dufftown's town square, where I found I had a definite choice of routes to take. I could take the right road, back down the hill to the River Spey and on 13 miles to the town of Elgin, where there was a cycle shop. Or I could continue straight ahead for Tomintoul, 20 miles away, trying to see how far I could get before Braw Handsel struck again. I thought that if I could just get over the hill beyond Tomintoul, I would be relatively safe, near bus transportation to Aberdeen.

I hung around that town square for at least half an hour, trying to make up my mind what to do, unaware that Braw Handsel was intending to give me 68 trouble-free miles through this day, and another 19 the following day, clear into Aberdeen. Finally, I decided to just test the cycle out a little, and happened to conduct the test up the road away from town, heading for Tomintoul.

You may have noticed that whenever you stand near the base of a tall tree or building and look up at it, it seems as if it is toppling over on you. In exactly the same way, whenever I looked down at the rear tire, it seemed to be flattening out. Yet mile after mile the tube still had enough air to go on. In fact, the tire appeared to be in the same state of flattening as it had been a mile back. In this nervous way, I climbed up the road past the towns of Favillar, Shenval, Tomnavoulin and Knockandhu.

Despite my fears, I arrived at Scotland's highest village of Tomintoul, at an elevation of 1160 feet, just before noon, and I rode into town aboard a still-functioning Braw Handsel. Tomintoul proved to be a pleasant little place, lying along a single long street with a square at one end. Its many little shops and tea rooms cater to people attracted there for walking, fishing and, in the winter, skiing. I wandered about, asking in this store and that if anyone happened to have an extra bike tube for sale, but everyone was sorry and couldn't oblige. I consoled myself with lunch, and then set

Castle ruins offer interesting views of the Scottish countryside.

off to climb the dreaded 2100-foot pass leading from Banff-shire to Aberdeen-shire.

Perhaps because Mr. Hughes of Thurso had told me how difficult Tomintoul was for the cyclist, I found it and the pass beyond rather simple to negotiate. I was "up" for something awful, and the awful became ordinary.

The other side, however, was something else. A sign warned "Grade 1:5," but I was flashing by it before I realized just how steep 1:5 would be. I managed to halt the cycle, and walked it the rest of the way down to an inn at Cock Bridge, while a light drizzle made the road slick and even more difficult to travel. I stopped for a sandwich (more like two pieces of cardboard with paper filling between), then rode on down through the village of Strathdon and on to the River Dee, the richest river valley of all.

My arrival at the River Dee was perfect. It was almost evening as I glided down out of the hills, through the towns of Logie Coldstone and Ordie, straight across the main highway, 93, and onto a bridge over the Dee at a place called Dinnet. As I crossed the river, there were a number of people standing on the lower side of the bridge. Curious, I stopped and went to see what they were doing. They were watching salmon fight their way up the river to spawn. Then, on the other side of the bridge and up 100 yards, a lone man standing among the trees began playing the pipes, serenading the plunging river and huge fighting fish with the very essence of Highland sound.

I listened for as long as I could, then pedaled toward Aberdeen along a back road beside the river. It was a pleasant.

I thought of riding clear into Aberdeen that day, but realized how tired I was as I rode into the town of Banchory. I found a B&B on a back street with a tiny room that was free, and took it for the night. There was a cycle shop on the main street, closed for the night, and looking in the window, I couldn't tell if the owner had the type of inner tubes I needed. (While Braw Handsel's back tire had not had a true flat, it did seem to require pumping now and then, suggesting the need for a replacement.)

Banchory seemed a far more proper town than any of the ones I had visited before, including Inverness. Perhaps this impression was due to the very nice homes I passed when entering the town. In any case, I felt very rude and crude in my travel-stained biking outfit among all these people wearing business suits hurrying about their important business affairs. I also felt out of place because of the busy traffic that filled the roads, leaving no room for the lone cyclist, making me feel in quite the wrong place.

I had to wait for the bike shop to open the next morning, but when it did the true Scottish country-squire type of a proprietor proved not to have the tube I needed. Two hours later, I rolled down the last 19 green miles to Aberdeen, and entered that city just as a torrential downpour began.

Wanting to get a general inspection and repair of anything that might be wrong with Braw Handsel, I pedaled to the cycle shop that had the largest ad in the newspaper. The repairman there wasn't much help, however. He just laughed when I said I needed the repairs done the same day. So I decided to purchase two spare tubes, and install the new one myself—an operation that by now I could do in my sleep.

Aberdeen is a full-scale city, with a history as long and intricate as any in Scotland. But perhaps by now I was in a state of cultural overindulgence —I managed to see nothing of historical importance in Aberdeen, and I regretted this terrible performance not one bit.

The two girls on the motorcycle that I had met in Thurso, Judy and Wilma—were both social workers in Aberdeen, and instead of seeing monuments I gave them a call. Wilma answered, and I invited her to lunch, but

126

she countered with an invitation to dinner at their apartment, an offer I could hardly refuse.

I felt rather strange, going to have dinner with two girls I didn't know at all, who had no reason on earth to give me a dinner. I managed to quell this feeling, however. For some reason I had made very little contact with any people since leaving Alison Leach in Muir of Ord, and I felt in need of good company for an evening.

It proved to be very good company indeed. Wilma and Judy had another friend over, who was going with them to a concert later that evening. We all ate in the kitchen, at a tiny table loaded with all sorts of good things to eat. Perhaps the best part of the meal was a jar of something called lemon curd, similar to lemon meringue pie filling, that went well on anything. All too soon the meal was over, and the good conversation that had accompanied it. We all said good-bye as we headed off in our different directions, they to their concert, and I for the town of Stonehaven, 15 miles down the coast.

The girls were kind enough to ask if I wanted to sleep on the floor of their apartment, but I felt guilty enough having the excellent meal I had eaten. I thanked them and explained that Aberdeen was too large for comfort, and with that I set off on my way.

Of course, once I passed beyond Aberdeen's city limits the light drizzle became a determined downpour. I was drenched, it was dark by now and the batteries were out on Braw Handsel's taillight, making the two of us nearly invisible to the cars and huge lorries that thundered by. The traffic was heavy, as this was the main road south to Edinburgh, and when the trucks passed they threw up great sheets of water, making me feel as if I were heading up a waterfall instead of along a highway. In all, it was a very unpleasant time.

I stopped at every place along the way that looked like a B&B, but there were very few of these. To make matters worse, it was on this stretch that I discovered just how spoiled I had become after two days of drifting down those river valleys. Just a few minutes out of Aberdeen, and climbing up a mild hill that seemed vertical and endless, I thought surely I must be near Stonehaven by now. This anticipation went on for the next two or three hours of endless work, without the hint of a city appearing out of the storm.

The rain and wind that blinded me made the brakes useless against the wet metal rims, and the water on the road made Braw Handsel's tires skate as much as roll. All the while the trucks hurled by, sounding like the juggernauts they are so aptly called, quite frankly scaring the hell out of me.

At last I did reach Stonehaven, my voice hoarse from yelling in rage and fear over where in the world the damn place was. Finally I was safe, and would be comfortable as soon as I found a place in one of the many B&Bs that were surely here.

On this night even the simple task of finding a B&B proved to be a bit of a problem, despite there being plenty of them. I knocked at one B&B, a woman came to the door, looked me up and down, and said she was full. This was a reasonable reaction, I suppose, as I stood before her absolutely wet and looked like a madman who had just been for a swim in his clothes in the middle of a stormy night.

The next woman in the next place also looked me up and down, then said she had only a double, sorry. I was walking away, shivering now, before I thought how strange it was that she didn't try to make at least the money of a single at this hour of the night. Evidently my drenched appearance was just too much for Scottish hospitality, normally so helpful.

I tried a third home, and on being rejected there as well I began to despair of ever finding a room in which to get dry and warm. But perhaps these sorts of things always work out for the best. I pushed Braw Handsel up a hilly side street, tried my luck a fourth time, and was instantly taken care of. The house was huge, with lots of heavy woodwork, and held a bedroom waiting for me that looked out over the whole harbor below and had plenty of room for hanging things out to dry. Hot tea, cake, cookies and a hot relaxing bath made the perfect ending to an otherwise long and wet night ride, one which I hoped never to repeat again.

Thirteen
On to the Plays of Pitlochry

T he next morning the rain was gone, but not the wind. It pulled and
pushed at me as I left my haven on the hill about 10 o'clock, and
continued to blow as I pedaled south along the coast to Dunnottar Castle.

Dunnottar is one of the most striking castles in all of Scotland. It stands
atop a great rock that rises 160 feet from the crashing surf of the North
Sea, connected to the mainland by only a single path that runs across a
deep chasm between. Today the castle grounds atop this crag are covered
by a carpet of green lawn, and the rough stone buildings that remain are
greatly enhanced by this gentle carpeting.

Dunnottar's history was anything but gentle. From prehistoric times
the rock on which it stands served as a stronghold for those who held it
against attack from the outside world. In 1297 William Wallace, fighting
for Scottish independence, stormed the English-held castle and burned the
garrison alive in a church there, where they had taken shelter.

In 1649, King Charles I was executed, a high-placed victim of the confrontation between Reformation and Counter-Reformation. Scotland declared Charles II King, and Oliver Cromwell came raging north to establish
control for his new-found Commonwealth. Cromwell's forces enjoyed
great success, until only lonely Dunnottar on its fortress rock held out for
Charles II. The crown, sceptre and sword of Scotland were protected here
in September, 1651, when troops of the Commonwealth began the siege of
the castle. Finally, in May of 1652, the English brought up heavy artillery.
The castle was forced to capitulate, but not before the regalia and king
Charles' private papers were smuggled out. (These items were buried in
Kinneff Church until the Restoration of Charles II in 1660.)

Two years after Charles II regained his throne, he renounced the Cove-

129

nants that he had agreed to observe in order to gain Scotland's backing for his cause. (The Covenant was a declaration not only of religious faith, outlining the form of religious practices at least a portion of the Scottish people insisted on following, but also a political manifesto, which in some matters set the Scottish Parliament above the King. The Covenant was signed into life by Scottish representatives at Edinburgh in 1638, and was a source of strife in Scotland for a dozen decades. The Scots believe in long arguments.) Once again, the blood flowed.

In 1685 came the darkest chapter in Dunnottar's long history, a chapter that still involved the Covenanters and the Royalists. One hundred twenty-two men and 45 women, all Covenanters, were brought to the castle and herded into a low-roofed cellar vault that measured 9 by 15 feet, or less than one square foot per person. There was only one window, no sanitary facilities and the prisoners had to pay for everything they received, even water. Understandably, many of them died from this brutal incarceration within the "Whig's Vault." What horrible things humans have seen fit to do to one another through history.

It was strange to walk around Dunnottar, enjoying the blue ocean beyond, the green lawn running between the remains of the castle compound, yet aware of the violent history of these very rocks and buildings. Dunnottar was complex enough that you could climb stairs to look around rooms open to the sky, and descend again, to view the empty vaults of horror.

The old keep of Sir William Keith is a marvelous building to inspect. Almost 600 years old, it enjoys wide windows instead of the usual narrow slits, with stone window seats that invite the visitor to sit and enjoy the meeting of rocky coast and crashing sea. Standing on the stone floor of the Great Hall, the visitor can look up to the next two stories, whose wooden floors are gone, and see the intricacy of stonework that went into this castle. Each floor had its own fireplace and chimney built into the wall, and each had windows and window seats. In another building there was an amazing room, a kitchen, one whole end of which was a fireplace so huge you could walk into it.

After leaving Dunnottar Castle, the wind became even stiffer as I tried to work my way down the coast toward the town of Montrose. The wind made the grass in the fields shiver and the trees roar. I pedaled along as best I could, leaning at a great angle into the wind to keep from being blown over. Whenever a truck passed, which was all too often, its bulk would block the wind, and I would then fall from my tilt toward the truck until I caught myself, only to be blown over the other way once it passed. Finally I gave up and simply cycled down the wrong side of the road, so that nothing could block the wind and I could at least maintain my angle consistently.

As I ventured farther south along this east coast of Scotland, I found the towns and cities more and more enjoyable, increasingly substantial but also very charmingly arranged. I also discovered more traffic as I went along, however, and a back road from one city to another became more and more desirable. Leaving Montrose for Arbroath, I found an excellent back road to follow. At one point it ran by an old red fort standing on a hill above an estuary. The structure was unmarked on the map, but still very impressive with its red sandstone blocks worn smooth and hollowed into surreal forms by the marine climate and harsh winds.

I puttered along, enjoying the afternoon, and finally came to Arbroath, a town of almost 20,000 which has part of its main street closed off so that the pedestrians may wander along it in peace.

Beyond the pedestrian area I found another cycle shop. I felt that my rear wheel had been increasingly out of true through this day's travel, and I wanted a competent workman to look at it. Several men were manning the shop, all in white smocks like doctors, so it seemed just the place I wanted. It was late and they were busy but one of them said, "Leave the bike here for half an hour, and we'll have things right."

I spent the time wandering through the ruins of the town's Abbey Church, dedicated to St. Thomas Becket by William the Lion in 1176. In 1320, Robert Bruce signed the Declaration of Independence from England here. Today the south transept and the massive west front are the most impressive remains from that time, their parts suggesting how magnificent the whole edifice must have been.

I was a little late getting back to the shop, but they were kindly keeping it open for my return. The same very nice older gentleman explained that the wheel was out of true because of the broken spoke—which makes 13!—that was on the outside of the wheel away from the gear block. Amazingly, the man had fixed the spoke and trued the wheel while it was still attached to the cycle. I don't know how he managed this, but it certainly seemed to justify the white smock.

I rode five miles down the main road from Arbroath, then went shooting down a long back road to the sea and right to the little town of Carnoustie. Here I found a quite good restaurant, where I spent too much for a very good meal.

After dinner I had just enough lazy strength to put in 10 more miles to the town of Broughty Ferry, a suburb completely submerged in the major city of Dundee, Scotland's third largest city after Glasgow and Edinburgh. Here I found a reasonable hotel on the waterfront overlooking a sandy beach, the hills of Fife-shire facing me across the narrow Firth of Tay.

The next morning I did a wash of clothes, wearing shorts while everything else went into the machine. When this was done I walked back to the hotel by way of Broughty Castle, said good-bye to my host and hostess, then loaded up and pedaled in to Dundee. The large city did nothing for me, however, except lose me on its circular main road, so I stayed lost and shot across the Firth of Tay on the high Tay Bridge. Then it was back to the relief of a back road and across rolling hills toward St. Andrews.

I was just going by a Royal Air Force field, perhaps five miles before St. Andrews, when something happened that was unique in my experience and stunningly powerful. As I was riding across the gently rolling hills beyond Tayport, I became aware of several jet planes that were practicing takeoffs and landings at this airfield, hidden behind low tress. They would climb up into the sky, make a wide circle out over the ocean, then come back in, disappear, then reappear a moment later and repeat the sequence. Obviously, they were practicing approaches and touchdowns.

I was much closer to the airfield when this pattern abruptly changed. Another jet, with far more noise, came boiling off the runway and climbed into the air nearly directly over my head—this man was up for no practice run. Instead, he seemed intent on showing the other pilots "how it should be done," and did he ever do it! After ripping the air apart above me, the pilot blasted the plane straight up into the heavens, enabling me to see the fire in its twin jets as it disappeared into the sky. Then with a plunge he was back, rocketing over the airfield at a very low altitude, upside down, following with loops, rolls and power turns at low altitude. All the while the jet's crack of doom boomed out over the sea and nearby St. Andrews.

This went on for 20 minutes, and I was entranced. It was like an electrical current running through me, every time that man-made machine cracked by overhead, exuding its exuberant raw power. It was awesome to realize for the first time what a jet sounded like at full bore up close; it was beautiful to see a man playing with such power, controlling it so perfectly that he was able to carve designs in the air with it. Here I was looking at the modern equivalent of all the castles and strongholds I had seen through Scotland, a human creation stripped to the essential task of warfare. And I was entranced.

In any case, I was held there by the performance, almost as though I were seeing an art form unknown to me, which used the power and speed and deafening noise wrapped in a machine of war to carve arabesques in the sky. At last the pilot finished, landed, and I was on my way.

St. Andrews, made a royal burgh of Scotland in 1140, is a town that radiates a great sense of history to the visitor. The town is still fairly small,

132

The David Charity family lived up to their name and took me into their home as though I were a member of their family.

allowing its districts to retain much of their historical flavor against the in-roads of modern buildings.

On the outskirts of town there lie four golf courses of the Royal and Ancient Golf Club, where golf supposedly had been played since the 15th century. To my eye, the courses seemed extremely flat and quite uninteresting, but then, I was still thinking about the jet.

The town beyond the courses proved far more interesting, its heavy rock buildings somber in the afternoon sunlight. I walked the cycle by the crumbling old castle of the town, its main attraction a bottle dungeon, a 25-foot deep maw with an entrance at the narrow top, through which prisoners were dropped and often forgotten.

In 1546, at the start of the Reformation, Cardinal David Beaton watched the burning of George Wishart, an enemy condemned for heresy, in comfort from the castle walls. Two months later Cardinal Beaton's body was itself hanging from those walls, slain in turn by followers of Wishart. Life seems to have been so uncertain for everyone in those times.

I walked on to the remains of St. Andrew's Cathedral, the largest in Scotland, started in 1160 and only completed in 1318. The original structure was 355 feet long and 160 feet wide through the transepts, but today only the west and east ends still stand, along with part of the south wall. A few yards from these ruins is a tall tower, the Church of St. Rule, open for visitors to ascend to the top, which I did. I spent a long while there, looking out from my perch 100 feet above the ground. All of St. Andrews and the surrounding countryside seemed spread out about me like a grand map, waiting my inspection.

From St. Andrews I turned west, my destination now a small town north of Perth named Pitlochry, which lay two days away. I was drawn there by word that each year the town put on plays in the Pitlochry Festival Theatre, and that they were well worth seeing.

I spent the night at a small hostel in Falkland, just a hundred yards from the ornate Renaissance Palace that became a favorite seat for the Scottish court in the 16th century. The next morning I continued, looping into the town of Kinross, on the shores of Loch Leven, for a look at the small castle on an island in that Loch that held Mary Queen of Scots for 11 months.

I was just a half mile or so from Kinross, pedaling along in a rather empty state of mind, when Braw Handsel decided to snap me out of my lethargic mood by giving me something other than castle ruins about which to think I bumped over a chink in the road, and a few yards beyond that heard that tiresome sound, "Cachunk-pinngg," as the head of still another spoke went flying off like a bullet. Thanks a lot, Braw Handsel.

Actually, this was an interesting problem, and I could feel my lazy attitude vanish in the face of it. Should I turn south for Edinburgh, where I knew I could get the spoke fixed but would have no time to return to Pitlochry? (I had reserved seats for two plays on Saturday by phone before leaving Broughty Ferry.) Or should I head in the other direction, for Perth, and hope that Braw Handsel would get me there, and that Perth would also have a cycle shop? I thought about this for awhile, but there really was no choice. I would have to try for Perth, if I wanted to see any of the Pitlochry plays.

In fact, the ride was rather pleasant, as long as I ignored all thoughts of possibly having to walk Braw Handsel over what distance remained. There was very heavy traffic, as the main road from Edinburgh funneled into the little road I was on. But my route seemed downhill all the way, and I was quickly in Perth, a beautiful city ringed by green sportsfields, by the River Tay.

I found the city's main cycle shop on George Street, just beyond Watergate, and a busy but very nice man there said of course they would fix Braw Handsel and have me on my way. He was as good as his word, and an hour later I was off, having dealt with broken spoke No. 14. Would they never end?

Perth was a nice town (I could easily have stayed there) but I found myself energized, thanks to Braw Handsel, eager to continue traveling while my illustrious cycle—now fixed—obligingly held together. Traveling very well, for the first time in days, I quickly covered the 15 miles to Dunkeld, where I rested by walking around an incredibly lovely cathedral set down very near the River Tay, with green lawns, weeping willows and pines surrounding its roofless walls. Then I pushed on, to cover the remaining 13 miles to Pitlochry.

Evidently, on leaving Dunkeld, I was sailing into just too euphoric a mood for Braw Handsel to tolerate. I was enjoying the ride, enjoying my hard, rapid pace to Pitlochry and thinking just how nice it would be to luxuriate there for two days, escaping to my two plays. It was going to be a great two days of rest.

"Ca-chunk."

Thanks a lot, Braw Handsel. Spoke No. 15 gone, and with it at least one day devoted to getting back to Perth and further repairs. Suddenly, I felt tired and angry and discouraged in the face of such infernal trouble with Braw Handsel. I didn't even bother to get off the cycle this time, instead just squeaked my way on into Pitlochry, the rear tire rubbing horribly against the frame.

I had not realized how popular the Pitlochry plays were, having only

135

learned of them from a pamphlet I found in a hostel. The town was packed with visitors waiting to see them. It was very lucky for me that I had phoned ahead for seats, because if I hadn't, as I almost didn't, I would have seen nothing at all.

I wandered around the hilly streets above the town's main street, looking for B&B signs and at first finding none. At last I did find one, but it was full. The proprietors sent me back down the hill to where they thought another B&B was. This B&B was not functioning yet, but the lady there sent me back up the hill to homes beyond the first. At one a young woman said, "We do have a room, but . . . ." Desperate by now, I said, "Please, anything," and she acquiesced. I went to get Braw Handsel from lower down the hill, and when I returned her husband, in painting clothes, was there to greet me.

"Shall I just take my cycle around to the rear?" I asked.

"No," he answered. "We just can't take you. I'm painting and things just aren't ready yet." Oh, well, okay, if that's the way you want it.

"But I have some friends down the hill and I think they have a room they might rent," he said. And off he went, down the hillside. A few minutes later he was back and said yes, they would take me.

This proved to be the best development of the trip to Pitlochry. The David Charity family lived up to their name, and took me into their home as though I were a member of their family for a wonderful three-day stay. David was a school teacher, and his wife, Veronica, a nurse currently devoting her time to their three children. Soft spoken, kind to a fault, Veronica had decided to try B&B work during the summer, and I was their first guest. Their house was full of books, David and Veronica were full of good conversation and their children were sweet and hardly a bit devilish.

Veronica was horribly nervous over how to treat her guests properly, and as a result plied yours truly, and three other ladies who came in still later, with far too much food and kindness. Tea, for example, was a stack of sandwiches, a huge plate of cookies, and several kinds of cake. Not wanting the poor girl to work so hard, I told her in detail what other B&Bs were like, and how she shouldn't knock herself out quite so much. She would ask her guests what they wanted for breakfast, for another example, instead of just presenting it. Of course, I'm not too foolish, I told her about other B&Bs when I was leaving, not before.

I had tried to find room in five previous places, and here I was in the best place I was to enjoy in all Scotland. It is amazing how often things seem to work out well, no matter how bad they may appear to be during the working-out period.

On the first night, after the three ladies (one of whom had lived all her

136

life on lonely Iona) went off to bed, David came into his living room and we had a wide-ranging, two-hour conversation about life goals, traveling in Scotland and his career as a teacher. We also talked about books, very good books and interesting books, not just display books. Such a place always makes me feel at home, while a house empty of books makes me feel strangely uncomfortable. David had been a forester before turning to teaching. He spoke of how most of Scotland was forested up to 200 years ago, but then most of the trees were turned to charcoal, or burned to make room for the sheep. So in this regard the re-forestation programs were really turning Scotland back into something like what it had been, instead of making it vastly different.

It was very enjoyable to be welcomed so whole-heartedly by this friendly family, as though I were a missing relative rather than a paying guest. In fact, Mrs. Charity hardly knew what to charge when it came time for me to leave, and I had to press the proper amount on her. What a lovely woman.

The next day was one of the laziest of the trip, and very nice. After breakfast, taken with the three other ladies, I took the back wheel off the cycle, caught the train to Perth, walked to the bike shop and had it repaired in time to catch the 1:10 p.m. train back to Pitlochry. Unfortunately, I had mis-read the schedule; the next train was at 3 o'clock so I read in the nearby South Inch, which the *Blue Guide* says was "once used for archery and witch-burnings." I like that: a well-rounded sports program.

Back in Pitlochry I picked up some fish and chips for dinner, and ate in the Charity living room while talking with young Alisdair Charity about his future plans and the state of the world. A spirited game of Monopoly followed, hotly contested between young Alisdair, his older sister Alice and myself, until the game disolved on a fine point of real estate law. (Monopoly in Great Britain is different from ours: Boardwalk and Park Place are replaced by their London equivalents, etc.) Then the rest of the evening passed in conversation with the older Charitys.

The next day was a drizzling, misty one. I slept late, then got up for a short ride along the Tummel River, and then over the Pass of Killiecrankie to see Castle Blair in Glen Garry just beyond. The Pass of Killiecrankie is a heavily wooded, steep-walled ravine with the Garry River at the bottom, and here on July 27, 1689, a force of Jacobites routed a Williamite force, almost the only successful note in the Jacobite cause until Bonny Prince Charley returned to Scotland in 1745.

Blair Castle, said to be the last in Britain to withstand a seige, was "Georganized" in the mid-18th century, and today looks like a large, white-washed mansion. I found the ride up to the castle much more enjoy-

137

able. To reach it you travel along an avenue three-quarters of a mile long, lined and roofed by magnificent lime trees. I spent just a few minutes at the castle after traveling up this road, then turned about and hurried back to Pitlochry. It was almost time for the first of the two plays I intended to see this day.

The Pitlochry Festival Theatre was opened in 1951, and since then it has offered plays, concerts and art exhibitions to the many people who enjoy coming to this town during the April-to-September season. The Pitlochry theatre is a small but nice one, with a restaurant and bar operating in the foyer, about which elegantly dressed people were milling for even this Saturday matinee. I felt decidedly grubby in my normal, grease-covered cycling clothing, the only clothing I had. Luckily, the lights soon went down, and the first play began.

Noel Coward's *Blithe Spirit* was the fare for this matinee. First presented in 1941, this play is described in the Pitlochry brochure as follows:

> "An ill-advised seance violently disrupts the home life of Charles Condomine by materialising his first wife, the glamorous and mischievous Elvira. This play is firmly established as one of Coward's masterpieces, with Madame Arcati, the 'happy medium,' secure in the gallery of great stage comic creations."

Despite such a glowing description, I found the play, at least at first, to be creaking and tiresome, its comic efforts obvious even as they waited in the wings before coming on stage, Madame Arcati contrived and tedious. Things got better when Elvira finally appeared, but all the lines seemed stilted and obvious. I left the theater wondering if I had made a mistake.

The second play, later that evening, was *Lloyd George Knew My Father,* by William Douglas Home, and it made the day entirely worthwhile, not only with its own virtues but in contrast to the day's first play.

The meat of *Lloyd George* was also given in the festival summary:

> "Lady Sheila Boothroyd has vowed to 'do herself in' at the moment when the bulldozers begin to cut through the ancient family domain, thus creating a situation which her family finds perplexing and inconvenient in the extreme."

This really does not seem like much from which to make a comedy, but since this description tells little about what *Lloyd George* was about, it really doesn't matter. Lady Sheila, a fine and proper woman, at first amuses all of her family except her "Colonel Blimp" husband with her announcement of intentions, and then horrifies most of them when they

138

realize, slowly, that she is serious. It seems that her husband, hard of hearing, opinionated, busy with his papers and memoirs, could not care less. His wife can't seem to get any sort of rise, or protestation of love out of him. There is a wonderful series of interchanges in all this, even more wonderful for those in the audience who saw *Blithe Spirit*, since many of the actors were the same in both plays: it took me almost 20 minutes to identify the actor behind the crusty Colonel as the man who had portrayed the smooth Charles Condomine in *Blithe Spirit*.

The light comedy of this second play was brilliantly set off by one line, actually by just the sound of the Colonel's cracking voice, when he acknowledged that he knew what his wife intended to do, and in God's name, how could he live without her? She happens not to carry out her plans, the play ends on a comic note, the Colonel is back to his papers, ignoring all around him, but in that one line we have been offered insight into one man's love for his wife, and his pained reaction to possibly losing her. It was a good play, well presented, and I felt the money I had spent on both of the plays very worthwhile.

I returned to the Charity home, for tea and more talk with David and Veronica—Veronica in her own kitchen now, relaxed and telling wonderful stories in her soft, gentle voice, about being a nurse in a town above Glencoe. It turned out that Veronica was from Beauly originally, and that her parents were patients of Dr. Alison Leach. She said her parents spoke highly of their doctor because she *cared* so much. A nice compliment, and I was also forced to conclude that even in Scotland, it is a small world.

Fourteen
To Stirling and Almost the End

The next day, a Sunday, was invitingly sunny and wind-clear, but I put in a slow morning inside the Charity household, enjoying a long breakfast, a slow reading of the paper, a careful loading of Braw Handsel, then more coffee with David and Veronica. I was reluctant to leave the haven I had found. Finally, though, I could find no further reason to delay, so I said good-bye to my new friends and set off.

I truly felt that I was at the end of the trip now. Pitlochry was the last exciting thing I expected to do on my journey, and now it was done and I was heading back to Edinburgh. The trip had been so good, its first tentative days in Scotland's South, the break for the tournament in Glasgow, then the mounting excitement and challenge of making my way up Scotland's west coast and islands towards the north, into the Highlands, then across the top and out to the Orkneys. I had felt a sense of returning to my start as I descended the East Coast, but there were still enough things ahead, still enough sheer mileage waiting for me, that I really didn't feel I was at an end. Now, however, I did feel that I was coming to the finish. I had already traveled 1801 miles, many more than I had expected to, and Edinburgh was at most three days away, at the end of an almost straight run to the southeast.

From Pitlochry I ingeniously headed west to start my return to Edinburgh in the southeast. I pedaled along a little rolling road at the shores of Loch Tummel, then turned south over some hills to Loch Tay and along that Loch's shores, to a hostel at Killin, 38 miles from Pitlochry. Before reaching Loch Tay I rode by the mouth of Glen Lyon, a glen long associated with the Campbell clan, just as Glencoe is MacDonald country. The Campbells, enemies of the MacDonalds, were the royal troops who committed the Glencoe massacre. It was beautiful country, far gentler in appearance than the rugged region around Glencoe. Just across from the mouth to Scotland's longest glen, I could make out the remains of a Roman fort, or camp, telling the passing world that 2000 years ago that great empire had tried to extend even to this quiet place.

Two-thirds of the way down Loch Tay, as I worked against a head wind, a bristling little rain cloud approached and thoroughly drenched me. This called for an immediate stop at the next tea house to dry off, consume some tea and cake and even read a while. The stay in Pitlochry slowed down my traveling speed considerably, resulting in a long, 38-mile day. After drying out I rode quickly around the end of the loch, to Killin and the little hostel just before the town there. Again, the stay at Pitlochry had spoiled me for the hostel life, particularly for the life I found at Killin. Two families were there, with several kids who had incredible lung power, delighted in using it at all times while fighting, and whose parents evidently were stone deaf, as they ignored the whole scene. Each time the youngsters went rampaging by I had a serious urge to throttle them, but I managed to subdue this. None of the little gremlins suffered any serious accidents that evening.

The next morning I made an early start, driven from the hostel into a drizzling rain by the awakening screeches of the little wretches who should have been screeched-out from the night before.

I spent a quite indecisive morning, as I could not make up my mind whether I should swing to the right just before the town of Callander, to ride through that area called the Trossachs that I had missed six weeks earlier, or else continue to the southeast, to Doune and Stirling castles. I actually was pedaling up the road that led into the Trossachs when the look of the moist grey clouds looming over it and the distances involved helped make up my mind.

I turned around and rode through Callander toward Doune and its castle, eight miles away. The road there ran through an avenue of heavy-trunked trees, and an excellent wind from behind pushed me along at an excellent speed, as though congratulating me on my decision.

I was still dithering in my mind, however, about whether or not I should have taken my golden opportunity to see the Trossachs, despite pedaling rapidly away from the area. Evidently, Braw Handsel could stand such wishy-washy indecision no longer.

"Cachunk."

At least now I could be 100 per cent glad that I was heading toward possible repair, in Doune or surely Stirling, rather than away from it, as I would have been if I had continued on into the Trossachs.

Stirling Castle's western side adds nearly 350 feet of vertical cliff to its own impressive walls, creating a look of dominance unequaled by any other castle I was to see in Scotland.

Once again I was forced to continue to ride on the cycle, hoping it would carry me to wherever I could repair the spoke, before more spokes went and the wheel came so much out of true that it would no longer turn. I pedaled on to the little town of Doune and decided to take a look at Castle Doune, situated on a green hill overlooking the River Teith, before dealing further with the cycle.

The castle consisted of a heavy tower and several other buildings grouped at the front, by the entrance tunnel, with a curtain wall protecting the courtyard to the rear. The guidebook to Doune Castle explained that this represents a new concept in castle construction, reflecting a change in the feudal order of military activity. The great buildings at the front are divided into two parts, without means of communication. One part, the tower over the gatehouse, was designed for defense of the gate and to house the ducal lord, his family and personal servants. The other portion of the front is an even larger hall, entered from the courtyard, which served as a barracks.

In the old feudal system, the lord could call up his vassals for only a set time of military service, usually 40 days a year. On this basis, he couldn't get men to guard his fortress on a full-time basis, since his vassals also had to tend to their own lives.

By the 14th century, the Scottish warlords found it preferable to have their vassals buy themselves completely out of any military service, through a rent, or payment. The lord would then take the money received and hire himself full-time mercenaries. With this system, the lords could have full-time protection of a far more professional nature. One weakness, however, was that these mercenaries might leave as soon as the money ran out, or might accept more money from the lord's enemy. Hence the new architecture put the lord into a private tower that not only guarded the gate but was also defensible against the inner courtyard, where his hired men would be.

The town of Doune seemed too small to offer the sort of shop I needed, so I set off on the six-mile ride to Stirling. The wind was still kind enough to push me in the right direction, so it was an easy ride, although rather harrowing at the end when I became involved in a freeway interchange while pondering just where I should be headed.

One plus for the ride was the improving view it gave of Stirling's most famous monument, Stirling Castle. The castle's western side adds nearly 350 feet of vertical cliff to its own impressive walls, creating a look of dominance unequaled by any other castle I was to see in Scotland.

In Stirling, the grade two hostel is in a building called the Argyll's Lodging, on Castle Wynd just down from Stirling Castle, and it is the only

144

hostel I saw that could compare with Carbisdale Castle for impressive architecture. Unlike Carbisdale, this house is truly historic. The building is termed: "Probably the finest specimen of an old-town residence remaining in Scotland." It is impressive in a heavy manner, a massive gate allowing the visitor into a courtyard surrounded on all sides by the high-roofed, multi-storied sections of this 343-year-old building. Unfortunately, most of the rooms in this former palatial residence were filled with a screaming mob of youngsters, all either armed with blaring radios or playing soccer through the halls. The warden, a wise man, had barricaded himself in his room, so the kids ran wild, prompting me to take several walks the same evening of my arrival.

First, I wandered back down into town, to Halfords, where they said I had just missed their mechanic, but if I would come back next week they were sure etc., etc. Discouraged, wondering if I could risk the 36-mile ride into Edinburgh—which I doubted as the rear wheel was about to start rubbing against the frame—I went back up Castle Hill, to look at some of the historic buildings that were near the hostel.

Just down from the Argyll's Lodging stood Mar's Work, 60 years older than the hostel building, a very heavy, very ornate residence that was never finished. It had a graveyard located behind it, while the front faced Broad Street, the town marketplace of old Stirling. After looking at these different offerings, and hearing the storm raging inside the hostel, I walked on up Castle Wynd and found myself standing at the bottom of a large parking area that fronted Stirling Castle.

To the right of the parking area stands a large statue of Robert Bruce, the king of Scotland, sheathing his sword after winning the decisive Battle of Bannockburn, which was fought just a few miles from Stirling in 1314 and in effect secured Scotland's independence from England under King Edward II.

To the modern reader, Bannockburn seems as strange and wonderful as any tale from the days of chivalry and knights-errant. In 1313, King Robert's brother Edward laid seige to Stirling Castle, held by the English. The governor of that castle, Sir Philip de Mowbray, in proper chivalric fashion, suggested that the two sides have done with fighting, on the condition that he would surrender the castle and town on Midsummer Day 1314, if he was not relieved. Edward accepted this sporting proposition, and in so doing enraged his brother Robert. The Bruce had very carefully conducted his war with England on the basis of never standing and fighting superior English forces in open battle. Now, because the word of his brother had been given, Scotland's King had to stand and meet whatever force the

English might send north to relieve Stirling, even if that obedience to the dictates of honor might cost him his kingdom. Amazing.

England sent an army estimated at 50,000 horse and foot soldiers to Scotland, as magnificently equipped as it could possibly be. Against this force King Robert could field an army of hardly more than 20,000 at most. On June 23, 1314, the English force under King Edward II arrived to the south of Stirling Castle, and Sir Henry de Bohun of the English promptly challenged a Scottish champion to combat. King Robert, to the horror of his officers, just as promptly accepted, neatly sidestepped the charge of de Bohun, and killed him with a single blow from his battleaxe. (Try to picture not just personal combat between the generals of opposing armies, but between the leaders of the countries behind them!)

The next day, June 24, saw the Battle of Bannockburn, which went entirely to the Scots. With great foresight they arranged their forces on terrain that would hamper the enemy, improving the natural position through hidden pits with spikes at the bottom, and with a good deal of luck they managed to rout the enemy. This sealed the success of the Scottish bid for independence (although years of battle still had to pass before the English were convinced of this). And according to the agreed-upon terms, Stirling surrendered itself to Bruce the following day. What a strange mixture war seems to have been, over 600 years ago, of gross brutality and gentlemen's pacts.

Stirling Castle stands at the center of a swirling history of battle and intrigue and important comings and goings, of which Bannockburn was but a single episode. Stirling Castle changed hands more often than did any other Scottish castle, an indication of its strategic position, while the fact that it served as the Royal Palace for over two centuries, until the union of the Scottish and English crowns, suggests the inherent strength of the fortification.

Since much of the history that involved Stirling comes down to a single word—violence—little that stands on Castle Hill today has much resemblance to the citadel that witnessed that history during its most tempestuous years.

I found myself greatly excited by the view from the castle walls, and by one particular episode from Stirling's long history. The view was superb. From the rampart on the castle's "Nether Green," the view stretched off over neatly patterned fields and straight into the heart of the Highlands. Only the distant mountains and the clinging clouds above them seemed to prevent a view of the entire earth from stretching out from one's feet. This vantage point surely must have instilled a great feeling of power in those who commanded from here, giving them a sense of being above the petty concerns that hamper the sweep of other men's lives. In fact, many of the lords of power who stood here seem to have fallen victim to such overweening pride, and time after time they appear to have been amazed when this assumption of superiority, even above fate, was proved false, usually in very bloody and painful ways.

The "Nether Green," with its astounding view, juts like the prow of a ship from the northwest corner of the castle complex. A wall of the castle, with several windows built into it, looks over the visitor's shoulder as he gazes out over the plains below, and from one of those high windows the line of the House of Douglas fell to ruin and decay, both figuratively and literally. In February of 1452, in the room behind that high window, James II, king of Scotland, stabbed William, eighth earl of Douglas, and had the body of Scotland's most powerful noble hurled to the ground below. There it lay, for 345 years, until 1797, when the skeleton of an armed man was found there and taken by the Douglas family for internment in their family gravesite.

James II, fearful of the Black Douglas's growing power, as had been Chancellor Chrichton when James was a minor, called William to Stirling under a safe-conduct pass. William came, supposedly alone and without the safe-conduct, contemptuous at the thought that the Black Douglas would need a safe-conduct pass anywhere in Scotland. The two dined quietly, then the king summoned William into an inner chamber. There he is thought to have confronted the Black Douglas with his league with the fourth earl of Crawford, the "Tiger Earl," which James considered a major threat to the throne. William would not, or could not, renounce this league, and in a rage James stabbed him. Parliament declared James guiltless, in part on the grounds that Douglas had not come with the safe-conduct in his possession.

William's brother, James, ninth earl, took a less lenient view of all this. He rode in force from Threave, bearing the safe-conduct, which he tied to a horse's tail and dragged through the streets of Stirling. Then, when he could not breach the castle itself to get at his regal enemy, he burned the town of Stirling to show his displeasure. (As so often happened, it seemed to be the commoners who suffered whenever their lords grew angry with one another.) This was the high point of the Douglas rage, however, although Douglas was to stay in revolt for the next 32 years. (As I've said, these Scots believed in long arguments.) The Battle of Arkinholm, in 1455, saw the defeat of the Black Douglas forces, and also saw the rise of the earls of Angus, the Red Douglases (another branch of the family), that chose the winning side and fought for the King. James Douglas was finally captured in 1484, and was pardoned by James III on the condition that he enter the Abbey of Lindores and remain there for the rest of his life. James Douglas died there in 1488, and with him ended the direct line of the House of the Black Douglas.

With this act of personal violence, James II did much to strengthen his position over the noblemen who surrounded him. This process was common across all of Europe about this time, as monarchs battled to establish themselves as superior to the nobles from which they rose. Few, however, could have taken such direct action toward that end as James. And how strange it seemed to me to find a thread of history I first encountered in Threave Castle, more than 1700 miles earlier on this trip around Scotland, tied off so abruptly by the fall of a still-warm body from a window in Stirling Castle so many miles later.

Yet Scottish history is like this, its actors and events forced to use the landscape of this small realm, until their history becomes tied and looped and twisted like a complex macrame through space and time.

Having enjoyed my walk about Stirling Castle, I returned to the chaos of the hostel. I was shocked to discover that it seemed the policy here to play bad rock music at the loudest possible volume over speakers mounted throughout the hostel. The noise finally went off, but instantly dozens of the little monsters staying there whipped out radios and tape recorders and managed to get them going at even louder volume.

I found myself tired and angry, not only at the noise around me, but also increasingly at the thought of having another broken spoke with which to deal. Because of that spoke I now faced a hard choice: take the entire bike to Edinburgh, and end the trip on a bad note of incompleteness; or else take just the wheel, and return to this madhouse of a hostel for another night. If onlu the bike had held together for just another day, I would have been able to finish the trip in peace.

With these thoughts racing through my mind it suddenly came to me that I was very tired of the hosteling experience. Then, for a moment, my mind also added, "And the cycling experience as well?" But the response to that was instantaneous.

"No, I'm not tired of the biking! I'm *not* tired of that. But I am tired of having problems with the bike, and of this infernal noise here. It shouldn't be like this. Because of that spoke I'm stuck with a broken bike, and now this noise, and I'm madder than hell. And this trip just shouldn't end like this. It deserves better."

Then another thought came into the boiling cauldron that was my mind. "Well, you could always go to Edinburgh with the bike on the train, get it fixed, dump all the extra weight that is breaking those spokes at Mr. O'Connell's, and make another swing for two or three days south of

Edinburgh. That way you could see Kelso and Dryburgh Abbey and Tantallon, and perhaps end the trip on a better note than this."

Which is exactly what I did.

Fifteen
The Last 100 Miles

I was at the Stirling train station by 9 a.m., still debating whether I should attempt to make Edinburgh under my own steam—the bike was still working despite the broken spoke—or take the train there instead. I thought of the traffic, and looked at the heavy clouds overhead. Well, I'd try it anyway. No, on second last-minute thought, I wouldn't. I bought a ticket and ran with Braw Handsel to the train, catching it just before it pulled away from the platform.

The ride to Edinburgh was a bumping, rocking affair, and as I went along I was able to convince myself that I had made the right choice. The day was gray and dreary, the passing roads appeared to be choked with traffic and all the country we passed through seemed quite uninteresting as well. Yes, I was glad to have decided to take the train. I also was pleased with my new idea, that of extending the trip for a day or two more during which I would travel without the usual weight on the cycle. I hoped that would prevent any further breakdowns.

It was extremely strange to be back in Edinburgh again. If it were not for the beard adorning my face, quite long now, I would wonder if I had ever left the city. Whenever you return to the point from which you embark on a trip, it seems as though that return immediately encapsulates the trip, making it almost unreal. Ronald MacDonald was there in his shop, and surprisingly he said that he had time to work on the cycle. But even talking with him served to enclose the past, with its 1884 miles of cycling. It seemed we were continuing a conversation begun just a few hours earlier, rather than one from months before.

Mr. McDonald finished replacing the broken spoke, and one other that looked suspect, about noon. I then hurried around Edinburgh's Castle Hill

150

and down Leith Street, to Mr. O'Connell's hotel. He wasn't in, however, and I immediately pictured not being able to continue on today. But I went to a nearby restaurant for a lunch of Ayrshire bacon—which I heartily recommend, in contrast to the Ayrshire countryside—in the hope that he would return before long.

Mr. O'Connell was just going in the front door when I came back to his B&B, and he seemed surprised to see me. (More likely, he was surprised at how dirty and ragged my clothes and appearance had become.)

He said that of course I might leave whatever items I wished. So I removed the shoulder bag from the back of the cycle, with the sleeping bag and the tripod it carried, took all of the pamphlets and books out of the saddle bags I had acquired and read, and also left several bits of clothing and other items I thought I wouldn't need as well. Then I said good-bye to Mr. O'Connell, hoped that he might have a room for me three nights hence and pedaled off down busy London Road.

Braw Handsel flew over the ground, and my mood flew just as fast. The cycle was fixed, I probably would have no further difficulties with it, the clouds overhead appeared to be breaking clear and I had three more days of traveling to end this cycling trip on a good note. Riding along now, working my way out of Edinburgh's suburbs, I felt as happy as I had the very first day of this trip, more than two months before. I felt almost as fresh and excited about what I would see along the way as on that first day as well.

From Edinburgh I swung through the town of Musselburgh, then past Prestonpans, where Prince Charles enjoyed one of his finest victories early in his campaign to regain the crown for the Stuarts. Here, unlike Culloden, his Highlander's wild charge defeated the Williamite forces under Sir John Cope, slaying 400 while losing only 30.

As I swung around the East Lothian coast, a huge power station with enormous smoke stacks dominated the countryside with its stamp of the industrial age. But after passing it my way quickly slipped back into a much older past.

The country of East Lothian is a low, gentle, richly pastoral land, framed by the pounding blue sea and enlivened with hills that jut up abruptly here and there. The little towns were of a most enjoyable size after Stirling and Edinburgh, their neat houses closely held by the surrounding green countryside.

At Dirleton I unexpectedly came upon one of the most beautiful castles in Scotland. This was Dirleton Castle, almost 750 years old, with intricate interconnecting chambers and passageways and stairs, which made me feel like a maze-walker as I wandered through it. Peering through gaps in the walls, I could see the castle garden, filled with colorful flowers and trees, bordering a beautifully manicured 17th century bowling green, unique with the ruined castle walls for backdrop.

In great contrast to Dirleton Castle, with its air of peaceful slumber, is the strong sense of naked power that radiates from the mighty fortress of Tantallon, the great red bastion of the Red Douglases, which stands five miles away beyond North Berwick. It was this edifice that I was hurrying from Edinburgh to see, largely because of a description of it that I had read in a fictionalized account of the Black Douglas family, Nigel Tranter's *Black Douglas*:

> "Tantallon made a sight to hold the eye, more like a vast feature of nature than any work of man. A couple of miles to one side, the great grassy cone of North Berwick Law rose high out of the rolling pastureland, and a mile or so on the other side the mighty mass of Bass Rock soared out of the blue sea almost as high, gleaming white with the bird-droppings that painted its frowning cliffs. Between the two, this extraordinary castle, unlike any other in the land, reared itself on the cliff edge, a daunting barrier of red stone, high and massive enough to seem on a par with these others. The stronghold was, in fact, a gigantic towering wall cutting off from the land an entire narrow peninsula of cliff. Higher than even the keeps of any normal castle, these walls rose, but at each end of them, and in the centre, three tremendous towers thrust up more than half as high again . . . Landwards of this imperious bastion were two great systems of outer walls, with towers and palisades and gun-ports, fronted by deep and wide ditches, one water-filled. There was no need for defensive works on the other three sides, where 200-feet high precipices dropped sheer to the waves."

Indisputably, Tantallon Castle still stands, radiating the power caught in Tranter's prose. It appears tiny in the distance at first, then builds and builds until the approaching visitor is dwarfed under its huge bulk, forced to wonder what giants could have created such a work on this lonely point of land. At a distance there is nothing against which to judge the scale of this massive fortress wall, but once you are beside it, it does indeed seem like an enormous cliff-face, an act of nature rather than a creation of man.

Once through that rising wall, the visitor is startled to find a gentle, sloping green running to a true cliff-face that drops to the deep sea

152

below. There is a well on this green, so deep that a pebble bounding off its ancient walls sounds like a bullet whining its way to the bottom.

The citadel wall is filled with dark rooms and passageways, and stairs that take you to the top for a view that seems almost the equal of Stirling's. The architects of this fortress, without Stirling's great hill to build upon, seem to have decided to construct their own high place, from which to intimidate the surrounding countryside.

In the evening's setting sun the rock of Tantallon glowed an angry red, as if to warn the world beyond that here still slumbered military might. It was easy to imagine a bygone day when that might was awake, in control of all the surrounding land.

Considering its incredible appearance, I found myself faintly disappointed with Tantallon's history. The rulers of this castle seemed more involved with intrigue than with outright attack and defense. The castle changed hands many times, was even besieged occasionally, but often the end result came through negotiation rather than military confrontation. If this impression in fact is correct, perhaps it arises from Tantallon being so impregnable that military force was essentially useless against it.

Tantallon was probably built under the direction of William, first Earl of Douglas and Mar—he is connected with it by 1374. William's mistress, the countess of Angus and Mar, secured Tantallon for her son by William and elevated him to the earldom of Angus through marriage to a daughter of King Robert II. Thus the Red Douglas branch of the Douglas family arose, with Tantallon as its principal stronghold. The Red Douglas line fought with Scotland's kings at the proper moments in history, and grew in power almost as sharply as the Black Douglas side declined after their eighth Earl's death at Stirling.

Finally, it was time to go, as I was the only one wandering about this stone rampart and the gatekeeper understandably wished to get home. I made a quick run along the coast to Dunbar, and there found a very nice B&B with a room at ground level, in which the owners were willing to let me house Braw Handsel as well as myself.

Because these were the last three days of my cycling trip, I found myself much more aware of all my surroundings than I had been throughout the rest of the trip, both outdoors and in. I deeply appreciated the large, comfortable room of this B&B, the excellent tea the owners offered me, the long hot bath I enjoyed later that evening and even that bit of television I watched. It was all so very nice, I thought, and I shall have to leave it all so soon.

The afternoon had been very good as well, a great joy welling up in me as I traveled out along the coast of East Lothian, flying ahead of the wind.

I had enjoyed passing through the little towns and the two castles I had seen, one ornate, the other brutally simple and efficient, massively impervious to outside attack. The art of the rockwork in these structures staggered and excited me, the skill in construction and the detail from the bottom-most wall to the highest roof amazing for structures so old.

So often, unthinkingly, we tend to dismiss anything from before the last one or two hundred years as primitive and crude, and then you encounter castles such as these that blast such an assumption to smithereens. Tantallon was old when Shakespeare wrote—as old then as America is today.

The next day proved to be a grey, drizzling one, and at first my excited mood of the day before deserted me. I had thought of going clear down the Scottish coast to Berwick-on-Tweed, but an uncomfortable drizzling rain and driving wind changed my mind. Instead, I decided to cut directly over the Lammermuir hills to Kelso. This involved traveling 14 miles on Scotland's Highway 1, the main road north from England, where I found the traffic not only annoying but dangerous. It seemed to take me hours to get to Grantshouse, a little line of buildings from which a country road departed the main highway and carried me up into the hills.

I was amazed at how my mood picked up as soon as I left the main road. Like so many freeways in the world, Scotland's A1 is a featureless, almost curveless and gradeless path through the countryside—it nearly puts you to sleep. On a large freeway, the next bend may be a mile away, it never seems to get any closer, and you never have the pleasure of having something suddenly revealed to you. As soon as I was off the A1, things nearby immediately became more interesting, and my enthusiasm for the adventure of cycling picked up again. This was good, since the rain also picked up as well.

I pedaled over the hills, then down through Duns and Greenlaw, finally reaching Kelso at about 4 o'clock that afternoon. The sky was still grey and dripping, and Kelso was virtually closed up and deserted because of early Wednesday store-closing hours. I had come here because of the Kelso Abbey, which I had read about. For a long time the remains of this abbey—the west facade, the west transepts, the west tower and two bays from the nave—were thought to be the remains of a small church. Recent work, however, has revealed that what still stands is only a small part of the largest and finest of the border abbeys. The remains were impressive, the fluted pillars of stone sweeping up from the ground and arching 45 feet above, but I found I was largely uninterested in the abbey's ruins. Nothing here compared to Tantallon, perhaps because the abbey is tightly rimmed by the buildings of the little town, and more probably because I

A strong sense of naked power radiates from the mighty fortress of Tantallon, the great bastion of the Red Douglases five miles from North Berwick.

had almost had my fill of old ruins. After a few minutes spent by the abbey I decided that I should continue on, in part because I discovered myself enjoying the simple act of traveling on a lighter cycle more than anything else, and also because I wanted to make my return to Edinburgh shorter the following day.

It was a very pleasant ride from Kelso to where I finally stopped, St. Boswell's Green. The quiet country road leaves Kelso, crosses over the rushing Teviot River and runs alongside the River Tweed, a beautiful Lowlands waterway enhanced by swans floating here and there in its slow currents. Just after I crossed the Teviot, I was amazed to look to my left at a completely empty, grassy field and small knoll. My guidebook said that I was looking at the site of the important town of Roxburgh, which in the 13th century was one of the four royal burghs of Scotland, along with Edinburgh, Stirling and Berwick. There was nothing left. The Scots destroyed Roxburgh, then in English hands, after the death of James II (murderer of the eighth earl of Douglas), who died when a cannon burst during the siege of Roxburgh Castle.

It was a beautiful ride into St. Boswell's Green, torn dark rain clouds coming and going, now and then letting the sun shine through to the green land below. This pastoral setting was as quiet and rich and peaceful as any you might ever see, yet this land probably saw more fighting than any other area in Scotland.

155

Sir Walter Scott is buried in a corner of Dryburgh Abbey, a fitting place for the man who did more than any other to celebrate Scotland.

St. Boswell's Green is named after a large, tree-ringed common that is still there. I rode past it as I entered the town center, looking for a place to stay. I found an open store, purchased a bottle of milk and asked about accommodations. The woman behind the counter, busy minding her two energetic young children, was friendly and helpful. She suggested that I try back by the common, and said that there was a place there that might have begun taking people by now.

"Are you from America?" she then asked.

"Yes, from California," I answered.

"Well, now, how is life there? Is it better?"

"No, I wouldn't say it's better," I finally answered. "It's different. You have bigger cars there, for example, than here, but is that better? There are bigger stores there, but you wouldn't stop and talk with a person behind the counter there, the way we are." Better there? I wonder. More money, certainly, but a completely different pace is needed to gain it. By asking this question, the nice lady behind the counter made me realize just how much I had grown to love Scotland. Often when I'm traveling, I've asked myself, "Could I live here?" Usually, the answer is immediate and negative. Yet in connection with Scotland, the answer could be in the affirmative. In any case, I know that I had found Scotland to be the best place in the world for a cycling trip. (Of course, I am prejudiced: I've never made a cycling tour anywhere else.)

I pedaled back along the green, spotted the B&B sign, and knocked at the door. I fully expected to be turned away, but the very nice woman who came to the door nearly welcomed me with open arms. A gas strike had begun in Scotland a few days before, and all of Scotland was grinding to a halt as a result. She was booked full. However, none of her guests had been able to find enough gas to reach her place, so I was the only guest in her large, pleasant home. She helped me put Braw Handsel into her small woodshed, showed me to a large and very comfortable room on the top floor, then asked if I might like supper. She wasn't really prepared to serve any she said, and I really had arrived fairly late, but she would see what she could do. An instant later she was rushing out of her kitchen with soup, chips and catsup, two poached eggs, toast, tea and dessert. Not a bad meal when I expected to get none at all.

After dinner I looked outside, and found a clear, blue sky while around St. Boswell's Common the trees stood tall and green, their leaves backlit by the setting sun. I hoped that the last day of my trip might also be clear, and with that I went up for my last night's rest on the road, enjoying almost the best night's sleep of my entire trip.

The next morning I woke to a knock on the door, glad for the night's sleep but sorry that it brought me to my final day of biking. Outside, the morning was windy, with towering cumulonimbus clouds gracing the sky. Today I hoped to see Dryburgh Abbey, then make my way back to Edinburgh. I had a long, leisurely breakfast, knowing that unlike so many others I had enjoyed along the way, this would be the last one of this trip.

The remains of Dryburgh Abbey lie surrounded by a stand of trees, which in turn is surrounded by a loop of the gentle River Tweed. The abbey dates back to 1150, but was destroyed several times by the English and finally left as it was in 1544. The abbey is not very large, but it is very beautiful, especially on a warm summery day. Sir Walter Scott is buried in a corner of the church, a fitting place for the man who did more than any other to celebrate Scotland.

I spent almost an hour wandering around the abbey. There was not a great deal to see in the ruin itself, but the tranquil combination of the abbey's remaining stone walls resting on green lawns, its rustling trees and the clouds passing overhead, all made a constantly changing tableau calling gently to the visitor to stop and quietly contemplate the scene.

The calm mood here was so pervasive that I even found myself taking photos of Braw Handsel leaning against a wall. Braw Handsel really was a beautiful cycle, I realized again, and I felt willing to forgive all the headaches he had given me. (Particularly since I knew perfectly well that the

157

main cause for these problems had been the amount of weight I had asked Braw Handsel to carry.)

When I was about to leave, I asked the keeper of the abbey about a statue I had read about in the guidebook, a sandstone statue of William Wallace, erected in 1814 on a nearby hill. The good man assured me that the statue was indeed close by, explained how to get there, then naturally went on to explain in detail how I should make my way clear into Edinburgh. I walked Braw Handsel up the steep road a short way, then turned off onto a narrow footpath slanting up a side of a heavily forested hill.

As I walked up the path a rain squall came rushing up from the direction of the Eildon Hills—the same hills I had first seen many weeks before, on my first day's ride to Melrose Abbey. The trees that arched over the faint trail kept most of the water away from the path, and soon I found the statue. It was huge and very rough, looking sternly out over the Tweed to the Eildons beyond. I wanted a photo, but the rainclouds overhead blocked too much sun, so I settled down against a tree and waited for the rain to pass. As I sat there, a series of rambling thoughts wandered through my mind.

The path that I had used to reach the Wallace statue had been completely unmarked, overgrown by surrounding vegetation, and the statue itself was simply there, hidden among the trees. In a similar way, the passing years have overgrown the trail that leads back to the men—like Wallace, with his rebellion against English dominance—who shaped Scotland's history. Yet with a little work, the hidden trail back can be uncovered, and at its end you find the men still there, their importance carved into the sandstone and granite of the history that they helped build and shape.

The rain storm overhead was violent, and in that respect was very like so many storms that have swept over Scotland throughout its history, storms made between men of differing ideas about religion or power or personal property. During either sort of storm, the prudent traveler or common person would have to hide under a convenient tree, if he meant to avoid the drenching—or worse.

On this three-day "coda" to my cycling trip around Scotland, I had seen Dryburgh and Tantallon, Dirleton and Kelso, houses of God and houses of militant men, and both of the latter surely played equal roles in shaping Scotland. The storm and the sum, the battle fortress and the house of worship, the Highland kilts and Lowland sheep, they all went into Scotland's creation, often in violent opposition to one another, making Scotland's creation a tempestuous one.

At last the final drops of rain pattered down into the trees over my head. I took my photo of Wallace standing there in watch over the land he helped father, and then I proceeded on my way.

Five hours later I was back in Edinburgh, and my cycling trip around Scotland was completed.

Sixteen
Postscript

T wo days after I returned to Edinburgh, Braw Handsel passed out of my ownership, into that of Frank Howie, the architect I met at the Maeshowe in the Orkneys. Braw Handsel had carried me 2002 miles through Scotland, and on that account I was sorry to see him go. Braw Handsel had also supplied me with one blown tube, one oozing tube, seven flats, 16 broken spokes and innumerable thrown chains and slipped gear levers, all delivered with a certain malicious glee and timing, all of which kept my sorrow at seeing him go from looming too large around me. As I handed over the keys to the lock, though, I couldn't help but admit that Braw Handsel was a beautiful bike, leaning against an iron gate in the afternoon sun. May he carry Mr. Howie in comfort and good repair.

I rode the train south from Edinburgh, looking out the window at the land I so recently had been pedaling through. At Newcastle, which is in England, I changed trains, getting off this second one a bit later at a little town called Bardon Mill. From there, a day later, I walked several miles north, to Housestead's Fort, or more correctly, Vercovicium. This is one of the wall forts that the Romans built, along with Hadrian's wall, beginning A.D. 122. The idea behind the wall was to close off all the wild, warring tribes of the north—of Scotland—from the conquered Roman lands to the south.

To do this, the legions of Imperial Rome in eight years put up a wall 73 miles long, 15 feet high and 10 feet wide. There were milecastles on the wall at mile intervals, with two smaller turrets on the wall between. Behind the wall the Romans built large forts, or garrisons, which finally totaled 17 when all was done. In front of the wall, to add to the difficulties of any would-be attackers, there was a ditch nine feet deep and 27 feet

160

The Legions of Imperial Rome tried to wall up Scotland with this barricade, started A.D. 122.

wide. The Romans just did not mess around when they decided to build something, even if it was a wall at the farthest edge of their mighty empire.

Beyond the rock remains of Housestead are still some remains of the barrier to be seen. The wall here lies on the crest of a wave of rocky cliffs that break toward the north, its own height hugely increased by the natural walls that fall away below. From this point you receive a deep impression of what it must have been like to be a Roman legionnaire, stationed here at the uttermost end of the earth, looking out from your wall over the edge of the civilized world, into the chaotic barbarity that ringed it on every side. How strange that must have been.

It was a warm noontime when I was at the wall, and I found it pleasant to walk along the top of it for a mile or two. I walked along over its lumpy stones, and knew that I was in nearly the same space as Roman legionnaires had been more than 1800 years before.

The idea came to me that unbelievable ego and gall must have existed in the Romans to think that they might seriously wall up an entire nation, an entire world, when they found they were unable to include it in their own.

And then came another thought. Think of the vitality and energy of a people who proved so untameable that they were worthy of such an effort on the part of Imperial Rome. Scotland was magnificent and terrible, even then.

161

Bibliography

Two Wheel Travel Bicycle Camping and Touring, Peter Tobey, ed., Dell Publishing, 1972, New York

The Blue Guide, L. Russell Muirhead, ed., Ernest Benn Ltd., 1967, London

Illustrated Road Book of Scotland, The Automobile Association, Hazell Watson & Viney Ltd., 1972, London

A History of Scotland, J.D. Mackie, Penguin Books Ltd., 1964, Harmondsworth, Middlesex

A History of the House of Douglas, vol. 1 or 2, Sir Herbert Maxwell, Freemantle & Co., 1902, London

The Black Douglas, Nigel Tranter, Coronet Books, 1973, London

Glencoe, John Prebble, Penguin Books, 1966, Harmondsworth, Middlesex

Culloden, John Prebble, Penguin Books, 1961, Harmondsworth, Middlesex

The Highland Clearances, John Prebble, Penguin Books, 1963, Harmondsworth, Middlesex

The Kings of Scotland, Gordon Donaldson

I also found much information concerning specific sites and artifacts in dozens of official guide pamphlets and brochures picked up through the course of the trip.

The author among the Standing Stones of Callanish

About the Author

The idea of a Scottish bike trip was first introduced to Eugene Cantin in a rain-dripping, mosquito-surrounded tent in McKinley National Park, Alaska. His chess opponent, waiting for the next move, began to talk of the joys of biking around Scotland in the spring and the idea was born.

Two years later, in 1974, Cantin opted to take a year off from full-time tennis teaching and gave thought as to how best spend that year. He knew that he wanted to hike in Nepal again and that he would like to travel through Europe with friends. But what else should he do? How about that bike trip through Scotland? And so the idea took substance.

Armed with the experience gained from his previous long-distance bike trip—23 miles around Point Reyes, California—Cantin flew to England, took the train to Edinburgh, and there began what was to be a 2000-mile bike trip through Scotland. By the end of it he not only knew some of the pitfalls of a cycle tour—broken spokes, burst tubes, painful knees—but also a great deal about the warmth of hospitality Scotland offers the visitor. *A Man, A Bike, Alone Through Scotland* accounts Cantin's education.

Eugene Cantin is a tennis professional living in Marin County, California. He has written two other books, *Yukon Summer*, about a kayak trip he made alone down the Yukon River, and *Topspin to Better Tennis*, a tennis instruction book.